If the Pink Shoe Fits

A Golden Anniversary Tribute to Mary Kay Ash
Celebrating Her Fifty-Year Legacy of Creating
Opportunities for Women Worldwide

Doretha Dingler

Published by:

Brevin, LLC
Scottsdale, Arizona

ISBN-13: 978-0-98537-256-9

Cover and interior design by Gary A. Rosenberg
Produced by The Book Couple • www.thebookcouple.com

Printed in the United States of America

Contents

To the
enduring legacy of
Mary Kay Ash and all
those in the independent sales
force and corporate staff who
faithfully preserve it by honoring
her values and continuing to create
opportunities for women around the
world and to those at the Mary Kay
Foundation who preserve it by
keeping alight the flame of Mary
Kay's compassion for women
afflicted by cancer and
domestic violence.

Foreword

$\mathcal{W}$HEN MARY KAY ASH HIRED ME in 1966 as her Special Assistant (and the tenth employee of Mary Kay Cosmetics), I had no idea I was being given a front row seat to what would become one of the most innovative and successful companies in America and that my boss would one day be named "Most Outstanding Woman in Business in the 20th Century." Of course, working with Mary Kay didn't really feel like running a business because her focus wasn't on the bottom line (though she was one of the thriftiest people I have ever known), it was always on the people. Mary Kay genuinely cared about all those with whom she came into contact and she, in turn, was adored and respected by everyone from the lowest paid employee at corporate to the highest earning National Sales Director.

Erma Thomson

Working so closely with Mary Kay for almost thirty years, I saw first hand how she not only wanted those who joined the Company to be financially successful, she wanted them to succeed in every aspect of their lives. She saw her company as a family and that's why she tried to call or visit anyone whom she knew was seriously ill or was having difficulty caring for an ailing family member. In fact, as the company grew, those of us who worked closely with her had to keep a watchful eye to make sure she didn't sneak out to visit someone in the hospital before an important meeting or event. She also insisted that everyone in the Company receive a birthday card personally signed by her each year and when some executive made the mistake of suggesting that the sales force had grown too large and therefore this expensive and time consuming practice should be discontinued, she simply said: "That's not going to happen." And it didn't.

Mary Kay also wanted her unique opportunity to work for as many women as possible, no matter their background or personal circumstances. She wanted everyone to feel as welcome in her company as they would in her home and so, not surprisingly, one of my jobs was to carefully assign roommates for the Directors In Qualification ("DIQs") when they came to Dallas for training. I tried to pair women who had enough in common to get along (both having young children, for example) but were also different enough to be interesting (say from different parts of the country). In short, I was trying to make sure their roommate was a good fit for training week just like Mary Kay was trying to make sure the Company was a good fit for their career. I think we both did pretty well.

I know that Mary Kay would have loved the stories in this book because she knew that the right story could teach someone more than a week full of classes and inspire them more than the best motivational speaker. Not to mention she just plain wanted to know how everyone was getting along. Mary Kay insisted that she get a copy of every Director's newsletter and did her best to read them all. Like most of us, she loved a good story, especially when it showed all the ways the "Mary Kay way" was working for women from all walks of life and, later, all over the world.

So enjoy these stories, share them, and know that by doing so you are continuing Mary Kay's legacy of women helping women. That is truly the Mary Kay way.

—Erma Thomson, Special Assistant to Mary Kay Ash

Prologue

WHEN I JOINED MARY KAY COSMETICS "back in the day" as my granddaughter would say, the idea of a woman starting and running her own business, particularly in the south, was almost laughable. To look back now and realize that Mary Kay Ash was able to see beyond her time and circumstances and imagine a future where women could fully realize their potential if only they were given a "track to run on" and a little help from their friends (and mentors) shows what a visionary she truly was. Because I was fortunate enough to have joined the Company so soon after it was founded, I had the privilege of being mentored by Mary Kay herself, a woman I consider to be one of the true American icons, and to hear firsthand much of what is now etched in stone as the "Mary Kay way." As the Company grew, however, Mary Kay was quick to hand the microphone over to the next generation. Were she here today, I feel confident she would want you to hear the stories that follow as the modern, living legacy of her founding ideals. Besides that, Mary Kay, more than

> I had the privilege of being mentored by Mary Kay herself.

anyone else I've ever known, loved a good story. Especially when it had a happy ending.

Much has changed over the last fifty years, but a lot remains the same. Yes, we have amazing technology today that I and the other early pioneers couldn't have begun to fathom when we purchased our first beauty cases and struck out into the great unknown, but the heart of this amazing business, the "secret" that everyone is always seeking, is still, as Mary Kay told us so many times, "between the ears." Put another way, Mary Kay is a people business, and people remain pretty much the same even when they are video conferencing on their smartphones and keeping notes on their interactive time-management app. We may be better connected and better informed, but the wisdom Mary Kay dispensed so freely to the unique community of women entrepreneurs that she created and nurtured remains timeless.

> Mary Kay is a
> people business.

As those of you who read my first book, *In Pink,* already know, once I started taking my Mary Kay business seriously (i.e., once I received that famous termination letter), it wasn't long before I became a Director and, soon after, that my Unit made the national "Top Ten," which meant that I was "invited" to speak at Seminar. Well, terrified as I was at the prospect, that speech, "Keys to Success," must have made quite an impression, because afterward Mary Kay asked if she could make it part of what was then titled the "Consultants Guide." Now, I don't know if that speech was plain old beginner's luck or if I was just especially cognizant of how and why I was making every decision at the time (because I was so scared of making a mistake and disappointing my Unit), but it became the foundation of my Mary Kay business philosophy and the framework on which we built the Dingler Area.

I still believe in the power of those "keys" to unlock any woman's potential in Mary Kay, but over time I have reexamined my definition of "success." For some of us, it means ranking Number One among Elite Executive National Sales Directors, with all of the awards and recognition that accompany such a quintessential example of personal accomplishment in our modern culture. But for others, particularly during challenging times, success may mean just getting from one day to the next, and I believe that is equally worthy of celebration. The National making a run at Number One is working just as hard as the Consultant trying to earn her first car while raising two children as a single mother. And, after all, in this company of unlimited opportunity, that single mother may someday be gunning for Number One herself.

Mary Kay understood the difficulties women would face, even with an opportunity custom designed to help them succeed, and that is why she introduced the "I" story as a foundation of the Mary Kay community. She knew that stories of women who overcame hardship, rejection, fears, and self-doubt would be just as important as the traditional "success stories" hanging in the Mary Kay Hall of Fame. This is why Mary Kay encouraged me to talk about my termination letter at every opportunity; she knew that in

> Success may mean just getting from one day to the next . . .

any given audience there were women on the verge of giving up who just needed to identify with someone who had been where they were and lived to fight another day. So, taking my cue from the master, I have assembled a collection of inspirational "I" stories from women who I believe embody the ideas behind "Keys to Success." They are not all Nationals or even Directors, but what they do have in common is that they all have stayed with Mary Kay for many years through many challenges and are still passionate about the woman, her company, and the opportunity that has had such a positive impact on their lives and the lives of those around them.

> Mary Kay . . . can meet people where they are.

If you take anything away from these stories, I hope it is that Mary Kay, more than any other company I have ever known, can meet people where they are. As the bumper sticker says, "Life Happens," and when it does, traditional jobs often put people (usually women) in a position of having to choose between financial security and their personal well-being, families, or values, whereas Mary Kay was founded on the principle that "God first, family second, and career third" is the only way to truly succeed. I hope the real-life stories of these amazing women, and the thousands of unsung heroes they represent, will inspire you in the same way they have inspired me, by demonstrating once again that the Mary Kay way is the best way.

Best wishes and safe travels on your own amazing journey,

–DORETHA DINGLER

With Mary Kay.

Where I Started

> *"Life is a succession of lessons*
> *which must be lived to be understood."*
> —RALPH WALDO EMERSON

I WAS TOO LATE. With the door slammed in my face (at least that's how it felt), and headed home embarrassed and empty-handed, my Mary Kay experience was off to a rocky start to say the least. My girlfriends and I had arrived "fashionably late" at what was then billed as a "Wig Party" (wigs were very much in fashion at the time, and Mary Kay wisely capital-

Doretha Dingler

ized on this popular trend as a springboard for her new line of skin care products), only to be told by the con- sultant that we were beyond fashionable, were in fact too late to participate on this particular evening, and would have to make plans to attend another party. Embarrassed but more determined than ever to find out what I had missed, I made sure I was on time for the next party and ended up purchasing the basic skin care set (cleanser, skin freshener, moisturizer, night cream, and foundation makeup) for $15.95. I never did buy a wig.

Well, once I tried the product, I was so excited to tell everyone I knew about it that someone finally suggested perhaps I should consider selling it myself. So I did. I bought the beauty case and started taking a few orders for friends and family with the best of intentions, but my brilliant new career came to a screeching halt when I found out I was about to be given a new full time job: motherhood.

Being a child of the times, I was convinced that I had finally arrived, my destiny soon to be fulfilled. I had a supportive hus-

It was more like a nightmare than a dream come true.

band with a promising career, a new house, wonderful friends, and now I was at last going to become a mother. Check, check, and check went the marks beside my life's to-do list. When our son, Devin, finally arrived, however, it was more like a nightmare than a dream come true. Instead of having my healthy, pink baby brought to me in a blanket like the other mothers, I was met by an awkward, inexperienced pediatrician who informed me that Devin was not pink at all, but rather an ominous shade of blue, and that this was most likely due to a fatal heart condition. Well, as you can imagine, I was beyond distraught, and it was many hours before our regular physician arrived to tell us that Devin's condition (a stuck valve) was not

Devin and me staring at each other.

that uncommon, and, in fact, had already resolved itself so there would be no long-term, adverse effects.

Needless to say, if I was on target for devoted motherhood before, I was over the moon now that it

With Devin all grown up!

felt like I had almost lost the baby for whom we had been praying all those years. As for my "career," that Mary Kay beauty case lay all but forgotten, gathering dust in the closet as I spent the next eighteen months staring at Devin, and he stared back at me.

3

After a year and a half, however, I finally relaxed my grip just long enough for a fellow consultant to coax me into making the one-hour drive with her into Dallas for a Mary Kay sales meeting. When we arrived, I was astonished at the poise and confidence I saw in the women who had joined the company around the same time that I had (though they had clearly been doing more than staring at babies in the interim). Given that there were several mothers of young children in the group who seemed to be able to take care of their families and still do this Mary Kay thing, I began to consider the possibility that maybe, just maybe, I too could "have it all." And so it was that on the drive home from Dallas to Greenville, as I pondered the previously unthinkable (motherhood and . . . anything else), my oh-so-neglected career almost got its second wind.

> By all rights, this should have been the end of my short-lived Mary Kay career

If any word could turn a woman's life upside down more than "expecting" in my day, it was "transferred." No sooner had I located my beauty case and brushed off the cobwebs than my husband announced that we were being relocated from Greenville, Texas to Greenville, South Carolina where he would be receiving a promotion as he ascended to the next rung on his career ladder. So, out of the closet and onto the moving truck went the box labeled "Mary Kay" as I did indeed take on what felt like a full-time job, organizing and overseeing a move that would take us halfway across the country and into unknown territory.

By all rights, this should have been the end of my short-lived Mary Kay career. Arriving in South Carolina was just the beginning of my new "job" as I unpacked, re-organized, and generally assumed the responsibility of getting us settled into a new community while my husband focused, and rightly so, on his new position. Except that Mary Kay had one more trick up her pink sleeve: she tried to terminate me.

Arriving innocently enough in the mail, this epistle

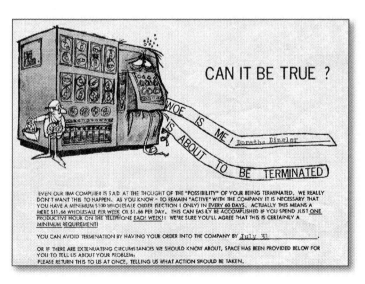

The infamous termination letter.

of doom announced: "Woe is me! Doretha Dingler is about to be terminated," and pictured an IBM computer spewing out the message as if the decision were beyond the control of any mere human at this point. The only way to stop the inevitable was to place the required minimum order by July 31, just over two weeks away. Well, as Mary Kay no doubt knew that it would, that letter shook me awake and caused me to set the first real goal of my life. I was not going to let some IBM computer in Dallas tell me what I could and could not achieve.

As most of you know, of course, I wasn't terminated. I grabbed the phone and started booking classes with two women I knew from my husband's company, asked the manager of the local dry cleaners to let me leave a homemade "Facial Box" announcing "Free $15 facial—Register here" on their counter, and doing anything else I could think of to generate the business I needed to place that order by July 31. Much to my surprise, however, once I placed the order and could, in theory, relax, I found that the momentum I had created (that one "Facial Box" generated forty appointments and twelve recruits) had snowballed to such an extent that within six months of receiving the now infamous termination

> That one "Facial Box" generated forty appointments and twelve recruits.

letter, I debuted as a Director with an incredible Unit that, five months later, ranked Number One in the country.

As you will read, I had other challenges to overcome before I could really soar in my career, but none so important as defying that termination letter. I believe it would fit neatly within the definition of a "defining moment" as I was forced to choose between my old life, secure within the comfort zones of wife, mother, friend, and bridge partner, and taking the chance to see what else might be out there for me. I like to think I took the road less traveled and, as the man said, "that has made all the difference."

With fellow National Sue Vickers and Mary Kay attending the first NSD meeting, which was held at a rustic hunting lodge (much to Mary Kay's chagrin) on Lake of the Ozarks

Work Your Mary Kay

"Life is not complex. We are complex. Life is simple, and the simple thing is the right thing."
—OSCAR WILDE

ONE OF THE BIGGEST REASONS I CHOSE TO WRITE a follow-up to *In Pink* was the tremendous response I received to the story about Mildred Caldwell in the chapter titled "A Single Mother's Story of Survival." Reading Mildred's story again, I believe she embodied Mary Kay's ideal of a woman who could succeed on her own terms if only given the right opportunity.

The Mary Kay world is full of stories (mine included) of women who were able to realize their ambition and soar to great heights of personal achievement. But for every Elite Executive Independent National Sales Director, there are tens of thousands of Consultants and Directors out there who either can't (due to personal circumstances) or simply choose not to set their sights that high for all or a part of their careers. Fortunately, Mary Kay designed her amazing company so that there is a place for everyone and for every phase of life (as you will see demonstrated over and over again throughout this book).

Sadly, Mildred left us far too soon and so could not tell her story firsthand. I believe she would be proud, however, that her legacy lives on as she reminds all the single mother's out there, and anyone else shouldering a significant family commitment on their own, that it's okay to "just work your Mary Kay."

Mildred

One of the reasons the Mary Kay business plan (used in conjunction with the Mary Kay value system of God first, family second, and career third) has been so successful is that it is flexible enough to help women improve their lives no matter what their initial circumstances. Put another way, it can meet you where you are. And no one could appreciate that more than Mildred Caldwell, a single mother trying to raise two girls in North Carolina during the late seventies. Though a daunting prospect even today, back then the cards were definitely stacked against her, to say the least.

At the time she joined the company, Mildred was working full time as a bank teller while also holding down two part-time jobs as a waitress and hostess.

Obviously, these were jobs that required her to be physically present (i.e., away from her children) at a time when no one had heard of flextime. Sick kid? Parent–teacher conference?

Mildred had been praying in earnest for a solution to her dilemma.

Tough. These were problems Mildred had to work out on her own if she wanted to keep the wolves at bay and provide for her family.

Then Mildred met Dingler Area Director Janice Hull, and everything began to change. Now, to really get to know Mildred, you have to know that she was someone for whom faith was very important, and no one had to tell her to put God first, family second, and career third. She was way ahead of us on that score. It should therefore come as no surprise that Mildred had been praying in earnest for a solution to her dilemma of wanting to be a good mother while needing to provide for her family financially. Well, when Janice came into her life (specifically her bank), Mildred knew that this was the answer she had been seeking, and within forty-eight hours of their first meeting, Mildred had a promising new career, a new extended Mary Kay family, and a new Director to whom she would become like a sister over the next several years.

If this was a Hollywood story, it would probably end with Mildred rising through the ranks and driving off into the sunset in a pink Cadillac as the Number One National Sales Director. But that isn't Mildred's story. Mildred's story shows that not only can Mary Kay meet you where you are, but it can take you where you (as opposed to someone else) want to go and still enjoy the journey. Mildred left her glamorous life in the food service industry and became an outstanding Consultant. She put both of her daughters through college and then paid for both of their weddings before finally remarrying, on her own terms, years later. There is no doubt that Mildred is a success story, but it was success on her terms and in accordance with her values.

> Mary Kay herself called Mildred in the hospital to congratulate her.

Sadly, Mildred died of cancer in May 1993 but not before qualifying for Queen's Court of Sales for that year's Seminar. Mary Kay herself called Mildred in the hospital to congratulate her and ask if there was anything she or the company could do to help, and that is the Mary Kay I knew and loved: the business icon who would stop and take the time to call one of her frontline salespeople to congratulate and comfort her during such a difficult time.

One of the reasons Mary Kay started this business was to help women just like Mildred who wanted to take care of their families on their own terms. Mildred's daughters have vivid memories of their mother doing extra shows whenever she had to pay an unexpected bill or buy something they needed. Whenever a need arose, Mildred would simply "work her Mary Kay" until it was met. Of course, her fellow Unit members also became a second family for her and an important source of emotional support when her health began to fail. On several occasions, Mildred told Janice, "Mary Kay is my life," and so many of us can relate to that statement.

Mildred recruited six people during her all-too-brief Mary Kay career, and it wasn't so that she could qualify to become a Director or to necessarily increase her income. Mildred simply wanted to share with other women what she truly believed God had placed in her life so they could have the same opportunity she had been given. And that, I believe, is the essence of what Mary Kay was trying to create when she founded her company. She wanted to design a business that any woman, in any situation (and ultimately in any country), could use to better herself and her family while still staying loyal to her values, and then share it with other women. I think it may be something unique to women that really makes

> I think it may be something unique to women that really makes the Mary Kay business plan work.

the Mary Kay business plan work. When we find something good, something beneficial to ourselves and our families, we want to share it, to "pay it forward," as they say, and help other women we think would benefit from what we've discovered. Today there are millions of Mildreds around the world "working their Mary Kay," improving their lives, enjoying their extended Mary Kay family, and sharing this amazing opportunity with other women. Just like Mary Kay intended.

With Janice, Tina, Joanne, Gloria, Bertha, and Robbie—
all of whom are featured in this book—at my Dallas home.

A Family Affair

"Never, never, never, never give up."
—WINSTON CHURCHILL

*J*STILL TRY TO LIVE UP TO THE WORDS of the song that introduced me to the stage every year at Seminar, "Accentuate the Positive," but on those rare occasions when I do catch myself hanging streamers for a pity party, I always think of one of the women I admire most, my first-line Director Judy Baker. Judy's incredible enthusiasm for life and the passion with which she pursued her goals in the face of a seemingly insurmountable obstacle (she was diagnosed with ALS [Lou Gherig's disease]), never fail to humble me and remind me how fortunate I truly am, even when life seems to be handing me lemonade by the pitcher full. Though I was acutely aware of Judy's difficulties, particularly as her disease progressed, and was present for many of the events in her life and career, it wasn't until I heard, as Paul Harvey used to say, "the rest of the story" from her sister Jane Parker (who has an inspiring story in her own right) that I came to understand what an incredible woman she truly was, and what a powerful legacy she left for those who knew and loved her. I know you'll agree after hearing Jane's story firsthand.

Jane and Judy

It was a beautiful fall day, and I was headed to my in-laws to pick up my two sweet children. I had been teaching since 7:15 that morning and it was now almost 4:00 in the afternoon. As I turned onto their street, however, tears began to run down my face and my soul was filled with sadness. *What is wrong with me?* I thought, but my mind kept repeating: *Is this it? Get up, teach school, pick up the kids, cook dinner, clean the house, do laundry, and then do it again tomorrow? I am only 34 years old!* I scolded myself. *You are so blessed, Jane. You have a good job, you married your childhood sweetheart, and you have two wonderful children, not to mention a nice car and a beautiful home, so why do you feel this way?* My life was good; it had just gotten a little mundane.

16

I wish I could tell you that I had a Paul-on-the-road-to-Damascus type of epiphany right then and there, after which I got to work correcting my life, but it didn't happen that way. God did, however, put a very good example of growth and happiness right in front of me. Several years before, my sister, Judy Baker, had called and told me she had joined Mary Kay Cosmetics. I laughed until my stomach hurt. Judy was an outdoor girl who hiked and camped and hardly ever wore a dress or makeup. But I watched from a distance as she began to earn cars, win trips, and take her life in a new direction with Mary Kay. Judy was, of course, well trained, so she offered to give me facials, asked me to hold parties for her, and even told me about the company as much as I would listen. But my answer was always the same: "No thank you, that's not for me." Looking back, it is amazing what fear will tell you that you cannot do. Judy didn't wait for me to say yes before pursuing her own dreams, however. She became a Director and went on to earn the first of many pink

> I called Judy in tears to share with her that I felt like a failure.

Cadillacs, sending us a copy of the newspaper article that announced her accomplishment. While I was excited for her, I still couldn't see me doing what she did. Of course, as I would soon learn, Cadillacs weren't the only perks Mary Kay had to offer.

As my daughter Rebecca was finishing 1st grade, she had one request. She wanted to ride the bus home on the last day of school. My husband and I were both teachers so we could not honor her request, and it upset me so much that I called Judy in tears to share with her that I felt like a failure. She quietly listened and finally said "Jane, I will come to your house (in Tennessee) and meet her." I remember saying, "That's crazy; you are in Florida!" But true to her word, Judy drove all the way to Tennessee to meet Rebecca on that last day of school. Her flexibility made a huge impact on me. That year when she and her husband came for Christmas, Bill, my

husband, said "Wow, you better check her suitcase. She is way too happy." The next spring, Judy sent me her Unit's newsletter with a copy of her paycheck from Mary Kay in it. I remember calling her and saying "I am so excited, you now make as uch as I do, Sis!" She

With Jane at Seminar.

quickly informed me that was for one month, whereas it had taken me all of the previous year to earn the same amount. Eventually these little "hints" began to hit home.

Finally, during a trip to Disney World in Orlando the following summer, Judy drove over to visit us and, after we had caught up, said "Jane, it's time for you to listen to the facts about Mary Kay. And you too, Bill." So we did, and at the end of the discussion, she passed me an agreement and a pen. I looked at Bill, and he said, "You probably need to give it a try." She then pulled her pink Cadillac around to the back of our van, opened the door, and pushed in a Mary Kay show-case! I asked, "Do you think I'm going to back out?", to which she replied, "I'm not taking any chances!"

Well, that was in July, and by January of the next year, I was on target for my first Mary Kay car (which, of course, my team pulled together and earned for me). To celebrate, that July the whole family piled into our soon-to-be-second car and drove to Seminar so we could all share in the moment as I walked across the stage to pick up my keys. Naturally, Judy had also done very well that year, so our seats were very near the stage.

I remember so clearly that, as Mary Kay took the stage, there seemed to be no one else there. She was talking directly to me as she said "You can do it!," prompting my husband to pipe in

> Life is exciting as long as you keep growing and challenging yourself.

with "Jane, I'll come with you next year if you can earn one of those suits." I later learned that only Directors got to wear "one of those suits," and though I had no clue at the time what it would take to earn one, when we got home I went right to work so that by the next Seminar, I could suit up and take my oath as a brand new Mary Kay Sales Director. As we crossed the stage, Judy announced to the crowd: "Never give up! It took me fourteen years for her to say YES!" I cannot tell you how many women came up to me with questions about why it took me so long.

I realized several things on my Mary Kay journey. One, when you surround yourself with positive people who are working toward goals and have big dreams, it is catching. Second, fear is only real if you let it stop you from trying things that you might enjoy. And finally, that life is exciting as long as you keep growing and challenging yourself.

Judy and I had many great times together in Mary Kay, so, naturally, when she set her sights on becoming a National Sales Director, I was as excited as her nine Offspring Sales Directors about this dream that we were going to achieve together! Then one day, I got a phone call from her, and she asked me if I could sit down. I could tell she had been crying. I will never forget her words: "Janie, I have ALS, and there is no cure. I am going to die." I was speechless as I held the phone. Finally, I managed to say a few more words that I hoped would be of some comfort, but I knew that our lives were going to change forever. The next few years were very challenging for everyone in our families as Judy began to lose movement first in her feet and hands and then in her arms and legs, but she stayed true to her Mary Kay training and remained positive through it all.

> "Janie, I have ALS, and there is no cure."

We went to Career Conference and Seminar on crutches and then in wheelchairs. When she could no longer bathe herself or comb her hair or put on her Director's suit, her offspring Directors were there to help, and it brought our Mary Kay family even closer. As she began to lose her speech, she hired an office assistant whom I helped to train to call her customers and answer questions for her Consultants. Because of her success in Mary Kay, she was also able to hire a care-giver to help with personal needs. She eventually moved to Sparta, Tennessee, which is only about one-and-a-half hours away so that we could visit and work our Mary Kay together. She was so determined to become a National that, to show their support for a dedicated Director who so clearly loved the company, Mary Kay corporate asked her to come to Dallas for an NSD interview. Of even greater significance, Judy was also awarded Miss Go Give, the highest honor that can be bestowed on a member of the Mary Kay sales force, by her peers at Seminar that year. Even as her body stopped working, she never did. The idea of helping other women find their dreams continued to fuel Judy's will to live.

In October of 2001, after living with ALS for ten years, Judy

With Judy.

passed away. I remember so clearly looking at the crowd when I spoke at her celebration of life service. On my left sat her family, which of course included her Mary Kay family. They knew her as a woman with drive and a loving heart who had been an inspiration to so many. To my right were her friends and neighbors from her church in Sparta. Many of them had never seen her walk or heard her speak, yet she made an indelible impact on their lives.

I also realized that day that all of these Mary Kay women were now a part of my extended family. They would continue to love and support me as my new sisters and help me perpetuate Judy's legacy. This year will be the twenty-second year of my Mary Kay journey, and even though I'm proud of being a six-time car driver and receiving all the other accolades I have accumulated over the years, I feel so blessed to have such an amazing and supportive group of women in my unit with whom I love to do life each and every day. You see, I finally realized why those tears came so many years ago. Every person needs a goal and a dream to make each day exciting and fun. To have a purpose and to be validated is as real as the need for food and air. I am blessed that Judy never gave up on me and continued to show me by example that I could do anything I wanted to do. I thank Judy for breathing life into me and helping make me the woman, wife, mother, and Sales Director I am today.

> Every person needs a goal and a dream to make each day exciting and fun.

A Life-Changing Decision

"A bend in the road is not the end of the road . . .
unless you fail to make the turn."
AUTHOR UNKNOWN

THIS QUOTE IS THE REASON PINK CADILLACS have to have such excellent suspension. Because Mary Kay is made up almost exclusively of women and, right or wrong, women often end up shouldering most of the responsibility for all the sharp curves and hairpin turns families encounter in life, Mary Kay knew that for a woman to be successful, she needed an opportunity that was far more flexible than the traditional, male-centric model that forced women to choose between career and family.

I've already told you about my first major detour, pregnancy; my second, our family being transferred half way across the country; and then, just when I thought I was back on the straight and narrow, encountering what appeared to be a complete roadblock, the infamous termination letter. I've told that story so often over the years, not to brag about how brave and determined I was (especially since I was actually terrified I wouldn't make it), but because, well, Mary Kay asked me to. I can't tell you how many times she would be standing in the wings with me while I waited to go on stage and say, "Tell them about the termination letter." If I hesitated, thinking to myself, *No one wants to hear that old saw again,* she would say, "There are women in that audience right now with a termination letter in their purse."

> "There are women in that audience right now with a termination letter in their purse."

Of course, she was right. Every time I spoke at Seminar, I was facing thousands of women who had some reason to quit, to give up on their dream. Whether it was a termination letter, a difficult medical diagnosis, divorce, or just low self-esteem, it is human nature to see these types of obstacles as signs and portents that we should pack it in and "face reality." And maybe that would be true in a traditional corporate job. *A promotion to vice president? Sorry, I promised to take care of my elderly parents, so that sort of travel and overtime just won't be possible.* But when Mary Kay created that famous "track to run on" for the women in her company, she made sure it had plenty of alternate routes and benches along the way so we could stop and rest when we needed a break. She knew that women, far more than men, needed a vehicle for their career that could handle like a sports car, haul like a pick-up, and stop on a dime. Then she painted it pink.

When it comes to navigating difficult terrain, former Dingler Area Director and perennial Cadillac winner Janice Hull is the perfect example of how a Mary Kay career can weather the never-ending pitch and yaw of life. When she first encountered the Mary Kay opportunity, Janice was very busy trying to better herself in the traditional manner but soon found out she was going to need a more-than-traditional career to accommodate the challenges life was sending her way.

Janice

I thought I was happy as an office manager for an optometrist. Unfortunately, that job didn't cover all the bills, so I also had a second job keeping books for a medical doctor, and one day, it finally dawned on me that I was working a total of sixty hours per week between the two. As you might imagine, the prospect of being my own boss (and setting my own hours) was something that appealed to me so I started taking night classes at a nearby junior college where I enrolled in the courses necessary to become a CPA. Of course, now I was working sixty hours AND going to class four nights a week AND teaching two classes at church on Sunday. Just thinking of it now makes me want to take a nap.

I first met Doretha Dingler while attending a skin class on a Friday night. Though I was impressed with the product and the opportunity (and her commission checks!), I politely told the Consultant who had invited me, "No thank you." The following morning, however, I went in to catch up on the books for my optometrist and ended up telling him all about Mary Kay. Well, I must have been more enthusiastic than I realized because, once I finally stopped talking about how great the company and the product were, he told me to call my Consultant, sign the agreement, and that his wife would be my first recruit. I guess that was just the encouragement I needed because before I knew it, I was off and running on Saturday afternoon with a career I had never even heard of before Friday night.

> I was off and running on Saturday afternoon with a career I had never even heard of before Friday night.

I was so excited I couldn't wait to quit my full-time job and spend all that time and energy working for myself and pursuing my new career. There was only one problem, however, and that was my husband, Harold, who kept saying something about how we still needed to pay the bills. So, to get him on board, I agreed to work a month's notice and pocket a few more paychecks before launching my business on January 1st of the following year.

Needless to say, I rang in the New Year with gusto as I celebrated my liberation from all those hours spent working for someone else and my newfound freedom to finally do

> In Mary Kay, it's okay to hit a few speed bumps (or a lot) and still pursue your dreams.

what I wanted to do. Of course, after all that time working sixty-hour weeks plus night school plus Sunday School plus taking care of my husband, what I really wanted to do turned out to be . . . nothing. For a month!

Luckily, I had put away a little emergency stash Harold didn't know about, so I was able to fund that much-needed time off while I rested and retooled for what I still consider a dream career, but not for the reasons you might think. Oh, I could talk about so many of the amazing experiences I've had through Mary Kay—the trips, the cars, being recognized as a Million Dollar Director three times (and counting)—but these things, as wonderful as they've been, aren't what make Mary Kay a dream career to me. What makes it priceless is the flexibility and unwavering value system of God first, family second, and career third that reassured me all those times I so desperately needed reassurance that, in Mary Kay, it's okay to hit a few speed bumps (or a lot) and still pursue your dreams.

I'm fairly certain that if my first career choice had panned out (becoming a CPA and having my own firm) it would have derailed when my husband, Harold, had his first heart attack and subsequent triple bypass surgery. At first we had no idea whether he would even survive, and then, after three additional surgeries over the course of four days, Harold's surgeon said that he had done all he could do and that it was in God's hands now (as if it hadn't been all along). Two prayer-filled and sleep-deprived weeks later, however, Harold was finally through the worst of it and strong enough to come home.

> That incredible gesture of love and support . . . would come back to me time and time again.

Of course, after such a traumatic event and four surgeries, Harold was still in very rough shape and needed a great deal of care, so I had to put my Mary Kay business on hold for the first time in thirteen years. If I had any doubts about the company's commitment to "God first, family second, and career third," however, they vanished when Mary Kay herself called and told me not to think about my business but to focus on taking care of my husband and start back when he was well. That incredible gesture of love and support in the weeks following that first terrifying episode would come back to me time and time again as Harold suffered three more heart attacks, another triple bypass surgery, two pacemakers, sixteen heart catheterizations, and an average of two bouts with pneumonia every year. There is no question that God wanted Harold, my Miracle Man, to stay with me awhile longer, and, likewise, that He put Mary Kay in my life so that I could provide for our family and still spend as much time as possible with my husband through good times and bad.

Mary Kay also gave me the flexibility to spend time with and care for my mother during the eight months we had together after she was diagnosed with ovarian cancer. I was able to keep her at home and provide for all of her needs, thanks to my Mary Kay income and the ability to set my own work schedule. That time together with my mother meant more to me than all the money in the world, and I can think of no other career that would have allowed me to do that. The same goes for the time I was able to spend with my five younger sisters, all of whom suffered from some significant health event that ultimately took them from me, but not

With Janice Hull.

before I was able to provide for them, comfort them, and love them during the time we had together.

Despite the time and energy I've had to divert away from my Mary Kay business over the years, I have still managed to be in the Circle of Achievement thirty-four times (seventeen of those being Circle of Excellence), be a Million Dollar Director three times (and the first in the Dingler Area), and win numerous Top Director trips all over the world (for which I still received the cash value when Harold and I were unable to go due to his health). Of course, there were also sixteen pink Cadillacs and a record monthly commission check of over $25,000 that the Janice Hull working as an office manager all those years ago would never have thought possible. The accolade of which I am most proud, however, was receiving the annual Miss Go Give award for the Pearl Seminar. To receive this ultimate honor, voted on by my peers, despite all of the distractions I have had in my career, was truly humbling, and, to me, just goes to show the wisdom of Mary Kay in giving women a career that enabled them to achieve their dreams and still live life according to their needs and their values. As Mary Kay told us so many times, "God first, family second, career third; in that order it works," and I am living proof of that.

> The wisdom of Mary Kay [was] giving women a career that enabled them to achieve their dreams and still live life according to their needs and values.

Feel the Fear and Do It Anyway

*"Nothing in life is to be feared,
it is only to be understood."*

—MARIE CURIE

*M*ARY KAY WAS OUT TO GET ME. That's the only logical conclusion I could reach when I received the special delivery letter asking me to come to Dallas and speak at the Directors' meeting because, as anyone who's ever heard my "I" story knows, my two greatest fears prior to joining Mary

With fellow National Sue Vickers seeking reassurance from the pilot of a single engine "puddle jumper" that was flying us to the first NSD meeting.

Kay were public speaking and flying. And now I was supposed to FLY to Dallas for the express purpose of making a ONE HOUR SPEECH?!? No way. Not this girl. As I would later say to my husband, I could see that being a part of this company was going to be nothing but flying in airplanes and making speeches, and I wanted none of it.

Later, fearlessly flying the Concorde from Paris to New York with Mary Kay (and, coincidentally, Mary Tyler Moore).

Unfortunately, I had a very supportive husband who offered to drive me to Dallas and have his mother take care of our son, Devin, so that I only had to face one fear on that particular trip. Of course, one fear was enough. I was so terrified of speaking to any size group for any reason that once, as a Consultant, I brought two guests to a sales meetings but was too terrified to stand up and introduce them. Later, Bruce would enroll

> Unfortunately, I had a very supportive husband.

both of us in a Dale Carnegie course to help me learn to speak in front of an audience, as well as arrange a personal tour of a commercial airline cockpit, courtesy of two experienced pilots, to calm my nerves about flying. And all I had asked him to do was let me quit.

Learning how to overcome those two major fears was a critical step in my professional development, but it wasn't the most important lesson I took away from that experience. What was truly significant was discovering that I COULD overcome my biggest fears. It gave me a new perspective: that fears were just one more obstacle, the kind I prided myself in going over, around, or blasting straight through when they stood between me and my goals. I started asking different questions. Instead of asking, "How can I avoid this situation?" I started to ask, "How can I learn to overcome this fear?" And that is where Mary Kay came through in spades.

The genius of Mary Kay was not so much in the company she founded as in the community of women she nurtured and cultivated until it grew into a vast resource of ideas, support, mentors, and leaders that could help almost anyone overcome almost any fear if she was just willing to reach out and ask. This is why the "I" story is such an important part of the Mary Kay culture. These stories are powerful not just because they often contain solutions to specific problems (though that doesn't hurt), but because they start with the admission of having a fear or a problem in the

> The genius of Mary Kay was . . . in the community of women she nurtured and cultivated.

first place. Mary Kay knew instinctively that women learned from, and were inspired by, women to whom they could relate.

I can tell you from personal experience addressing tens of thousands of women over the course of my career that the lights didn't start coming on in their eyes until I talked about my personal struggles. About not wanting to leave my newborn son, about not wanting to get on an airplane, and about absolutely not wanting to step onto a stage in front of an audience. And if someone couldn't relate to my story, perhaps she could relate to the National who spoke after me, or to the Director who was teaching a class later that afternoon, or (more likely) to the woman she was standing in line with waiting for the restroom. That is why we have to keep talking, keep sharing, and keep encouraging one another forward toward our goals, whether that goal is to become a Director, a National, or maybe just to sell a little bit more than last month to pay that unexpected car repair bill. We have to keep the conversation going, and so, to that end, I'd like to share the story of former Dingler Area Director Cathy Garvin, who knows a thing or two about facing one's fears.

Cathy

When I think about the day I joined Mary Kay (or rather, the day my mother told the consultant that "yes," I wanted to join and then handed me the contract to sign as she paid for the beauty case), the first word that comes to mind is . . . FEAR. Fear of the unknown and of not being smart enough to do this. Unfortunately, these feelings were all too familiar because, though I felt like I couldn't talk about it at the time, I was in an abusive marriage where feeling afraid had become the status quo. I was miserable, with no self-esteem and no self-worth. Worst of all, I was too afraid to do anything about my situation.

Despite everything, I still hung on to my little-girl fantasy: to leave my hometown with its very limited opportunities, spread my wings, and see the world. I mean, after all, a girl can dream, right? But most of the time, it seemed like just that: a dream. Still, when I was about as down as anyone could be and still function,

> Despite everything, I still hung on to my little-girl fantasy: to leave my hometown . . . , spread my wings, and see the world.

that glimmer of hope and my children kept me going. To this day, only a select few know how bad my situation really was.

Then along came Mary Kay (with a little encouragement, of course). I said "NO" but my mother said "YES." Mom had no idea how bad things really were in my life, but she did know I needed to do something different. So she purchased my showcase and then asked my dear, sweet, old-maid aunt to pay for my initial inventory, which I think was $600 wholesale. I was in business. Unfortunately, they were the only ones smiling, while I felt like crying. In fact, I was so upset with my mom for making me "do the Mary Kay thing" that I did nothing with it for months. My starter kit and inventory went into the closet, and, because my mom was telling anyone who would listen that I was "selling Mary Kay now," I had to avoid everyone we knew.

I also chose not to talk to this lady who kept calling me. She said she was my Director and wanted to talk to me about my new business. Was she nuts? I didn't have any business to discuss, but she was persistent. My recruiter, who eventually became one of my best friends and mentors, was also calling me on a regular basis to tell me that I could do this business, but I needed to do SOMETHING. Well, after several months of ignoring her advice, my recruiter called to inform me that she was going to be in town to visit her parents and that I was to have five women in my home so she could show me how to actually " 'do' this Mary Kay thing."

I felt like the little country mouse that came to the big city.

For once, I followed instructions. I invited five friends and watched as my recruiter treated them to a Mary Kay facial, after which they handed her CASH for products to take home with them. I was shocked to say the least. I didn't expect anyone would buy any of that stuff, but they loved it. In my mind, I thought, *Well, if she could do that, there might be possibilities for me.* I still was not totally on the Mary Kay bandwagon, however. I was curious, but I let fear, that constant companion, and my home situation hold me back.

This thing called Seminar was coming up, however, and my Director was calling to see if I had mailed my registration. She said I simply had to be there, and when talking to me didn't work she went over my head. She called my mom, and the two of them decided I was going to Seminar in Dallas, Texas. And sure enough, come July my parents, my aunt, and my three-year-old daughter piled into the car and struck out west for Seminar. Then my real Mary Kay journey began.

When we drove up to the Fairmont Hotel in Dallas, me in my cotton skirt and blouse, I was in total amazement. There were drop-dead-gorgeous women everywhere, dressed and made up to perfection, and then there was me. I felt like the little country mouse that came to the big city where everyone knew she didn't belong. I am not usually a cry baby, but, on this day, after finally getting checked into the hotel and still in total awe of my surroundings, I got on the elevator with one of those impeccably dressed women who was looking so perfect and professional in that suit so many of them were wearing, and I could feel the tears burning my cheeks. When she asked what was wrong, I told her I had no business being here. I wasn't dressed like everyone else and didn't know anything about Mary Kay. Then, to my complete surprise, she put her arms around me and said, "God has reasons for you being here. You become a sponge and soak up everything that you possibly can, and you will not be sorry that you came. You are beautiful." Then the elevator opened, and she was gone. It just so happened that this Director, Jean McMackin, was in my national Area, and she and I would later develop a wonderful friendship. I have told her many times that she saved my life in that elevator.

> I can honestly say that something wonderful happened to me at that first seminar.

I did soak up everything I could at that first Seminar. I learned that I was "prize motivated" as I watched all different types of women receiving awards for their accomplishments. And they were not the "Barbie" type either; they were real women just like me. Looking back, I can honestly say that something wonderful happened to me at that first seminar—I caught a vision of what my life could be if I chose to do something with it. I realized that my little-girl dream could actually come true, and I decided right then and there that I would be on stage at the next Seminar, if for no other reason than I wanted one of those diamond rings (because there was certainly no money for such extravagances in my world back home). I remember making the statement to another Consultant I met, who has since become one of my best girl-friends ever, that I would be on stage next year getting one of those rings. She looked me in the eye and said "I do believe you will." Of course, I had no clue how to go about earning that particular piece of jewelry, but I knew I had to have it.

Well, I'm happy to report that I did earn one of those

diamond rings at Seminar the next year AND was on stage to receive the keys to my first Mary Kay car AND debuted as a Director! Amazing what a little bit of vision can do for someone. Shortly afterward, with counseling and the support of my Mary Kay family, I finally mustered the courage to file for divorce, after which I soared even more in my business and actually began to enjoy quality time with my family. Life was good.

A few years later, I decided to try the marriage thing again, and I was so very fortunate to have Mary Kay Ash make a surprise appearance at my wedding in Dallas. It was truly my fairy tale. I was to have several precious moments with Mary Kay during this time of my life, and, for those who were for-

Mary Kay with Cathy.

tunate enough to have known her and spent time with her, you know how very special those times were. When she put her little hands lovingly on your cheeks and looked into your eyes, you felt like you were the only other person on the planet. Each time we would talk, I would attempt to say, "Thank you, Mary Kay, for all the ways my life has changed for the better," but by the time I got past "thank you," tears were rolling down my cheeks. She would just pat my hand and say, "I know." What a woman. What a role model.

Over the course of my career I have (so far) been in the

Queen's Court of Sales four times, been number six in the Queen's Court of Recruiting, and, of course, earned the pink Caddy—my trophy on wheels. I also got to travel to Europe with my new husband, something I had always wanted to do, and was even given the opportunity to have dinner with the president of Mary Kay Germany and his wife. I was living my little-girl dream and loving it. I was setting goals for myself and for my Unit and accomplishing things I had only ever dreamed of. I really had to pinch myself at times to make sure I wasn't dreaming!

With Cathy at Awards Night.

Of course, life still happens outside the "Pink Bubble." My Senior Director, Judy Baker, was diagnosed with a terminal illness, my "perfect" marriage ultimately ended in divorce, and my middle daughter was in a terrible car accident that left her with permanent neurological damage. These were, and are, difficult events, but through it all my Mary Kay family has been there to help me celebrate the good times and comfort me during the bad. Most importantly, I am no longer afraid of life. Mary Kay has shown me that I can and will get through whatever challenges life throws at me and still succeed on my own terms. And for that I will be forever grateful.

How to Silence the Still, Small, Negative Voice

*"If you hear a voice within you say
'you cannot paint,' then by all means paint,
and that voice will be silenced."*
—VINCENT VAN GOGH

OLD TURKEY. THAT'S HOW I QUIT SMOKING once I realized how dangerous it was to my health, but it revealed something more. Even though I only smoked socially while playing bridge (after all, my inner teenager argued, "Everyone else was doing it"), once I stopped I realized that I felt better about myself. My self-esteem actually improved once I quit, which told me that smoking had been making me feel less-than, and I hadn't even known it. And that's the problem with a lot of self-esteem issues: they can lie just beneath the surface and cause us to doubt ourselves, to give up on things we could otherwise achieve, and to generally feel lousy when we should be excited about who we are and what we can accomplish.

I talked about fear earlier and about how important it is to face our fears and learn to manage them, but, as difficult as that task can be, at least we know the fear is there. When I had to address an audience in the early days of my career, I knew I was afraid of public speaking because my hands were shaking and my

Facing my fear of public speaking.

heart was beating out of my chest. Self-esteem issues, however, can blindside us such that we end up bruised and battered on the side of the road with no idea what hit us or how to avoid it in the future. After all, if we didn't get the license plate number of the "I'm not smart enough to do this" truck, it'll get us every time.

I believe women are particularly vulnerable to self-esteem issues, and, though I agree wholeheartedly with Mary Kay's assessment that "Two years in this business is like a degree in psychology and four years a Ph.D.," I'm not going to try and diagnose why we seem to be so susceptible but instead get straight to writing the prescription. Just as when we were addressing our fears, the answer begins with listening, really listening, to the "I" stories of those women all around us who make up the

Mary Kay community. By listening to those who have identified, struggled with, and (most days) overcome those self-critical voices in their subconscious, we can learn to recognize when our own words and actions are actually blinking lights on the cognitive dashboard telling us we are in desperate need of a tune-up.

I am reminded of a trip I took to Florida one year during which one of the Director's husbands invited my son, Devin, to come along on a lobster diving expedition. Everyone had a great time, and we ate lobster for a week, but, as Devin tells it, before he could make his first catch, he had to learn how to actually find those pesky crimson crustaceans. Apparently, lobsters like to spend most of their time under rocks and ledges, safe from the eyes of predators swimming overhead, with only their antennae sticking out to warn them if danger is approaching. The lobster diver therefore has to learn to distinguish lobster antennae from among all of the other spiky things protruding from the sea floor so he can swoop down and coax the lobster into his net. Well, Devin said it took most of the first day before he finally learned to "see" those antennae by watching the other divers, but once his visual perception finally clicked into lobster mode,

> We can learn to recognize when our own words and actions are actually blinking lights on the cognitive dashboard.

he realized they had been all around him the entire time.

This story has become shorthand in our family for learning to see something right in front of you that was "hiding in plain sight, so to speak," and I think it is particularly applicable to self-esteem issues. We have to learn to peer underneath the rocks and ledges of our subconscious and see what is hiding down there hoping to go unnoticed. By listening to more experienced divers, however, we can learn to identify those thoughts and behaviors that are holding us back and flush them out into the open where they can be addressed. When we hear someone talk about a critical parent, spouse, "friend," or sibling who planted a message (or "tapes" as I've heard them called) that was then replayed over and over throughout their lives telling them "you're not smart enough" or "pretty enough" or "thin enough" or fill-in-the-blank enough, it makes us reflect on what exactly is playing on our own mental iPod. What risks did we not take or, worse, what opportunities did we sabotage because that critical voice needed to be proven right?

> Once we learn to identify the poison, the antidote is readily available.

The good news is that, once we learn to identify the poison, the antidote is readily available. Having based her company on what she believed to be the infinite potential of women, Mary Kay made sure that every event, most notably Seminar, helped to build self-confidence and replace those negative "tapes" with her mantra of "You can do it." From the cars, the trips, and the jewelry to the endless recognition and constant applause, Mary Kay wanted all of us to realize we have something worth celebrating. Of course, she also wanted us, especially those of us sitting in the last row wearing our one good dress, to hear the stories of how those standing on stage overcame their own "You'll never amount to anything" messages (or perhaps the deafening silence from those who should have been encouraging them) to get there. The true miracle of Mary Kay lies in the unique community of women she created and the never-ending story of how any woman from any background can succeed on her own terms if she can only learn to believe in herself. So, with that in mind, let's hear from someone who learned how to tame her self-esteem gremlins the Mary Kay way, former Dingler Area Director Shirley Monnet.

Shirley

I was painfully shy before joining Mary Kay. So much so that I would check to make sure there weren't any neighbors outside before I went to the mailbox because I might have to talk to them. Only years later would I realize the extent to which that crippling shyness, and the low self-esteem on which it was based, was holding me back. I was fully occupied in my roles as "wife" and "mother," and I loved all of that, but, as busy as I was, I felt something was missing in my life. I needed something more to bring me out of my shell. I needed to find ME!

Fortunately, I found Mary Kay (or Mary Kay found me), and I eventually discovered that part of myself I had been seeking. Ironically, I discovered that what I enjoyed most was the training and teaching. It didn't happen overnight, though, and I definitely had to go through some growing pains before I was ready. As a result of that experience, however, one of the things that I enjoy teaching people the most these days is how to realize their potential. After all, this stuff is just too good not to share! It is so much fun to take someone who has never worn make-up and teach her how to look and feel beautiful every day, but, beyond that, to be able to take a shy girl with little or no self-esteem (like me) and teach her how to change her whole life? That is exciting and rewarding beyond words!

I am happy to report that, as my confidence grew, so did my dreams. That shy girl who couldn't go the mailbox for fear of having to talk to someone became the final Offspring Director my Senior Director Doretha Dingler needed to qualify as a National. I remember she came to Charleston and invited me to her hotel "to talk about something" (scared me so bad I made my husband go with me!). Over breakfast, Doretha explained that she had decided to pursue NSD qualification and felt she needed a Director in the Charleston area. We talked for over an hour, but the five words she said that changed my life were the ones I had never heard before . . . "I think you'd be GREAT!" Well, I guess that was just the encouragement I needed because I left that meeting and recruited three people before the day was out. Needless to say my shyness was a distant memory after catching something more contagious than any virus known to man . . . enthusiasm!

I still marvel at Mary Kay's wisdom when she planned this company. She knew that I, like so many other women, might have to overcome fear and lack of self-confidence in order to succeed. She gave us a step-by-step plan and instilled her wonderful "praise your people to success" philosophy in new Directors from day one. I know that my Unit and I absolutely thrive on recognition, and, as a result, we have achieved Unit Circle eight times. I've also earned five pink Cadillacs, monthly commission checks in excess of $10,000, and even a 2,300 square foot suite in Dallas where I was picked up in a limousine by a driver holding a funny-looking sign with my name on it! Of course, those checks allowed my husband

> **Those checks allowed [us] to do things like . . . put all three of our children through college AT THE SAME TIME.**

and me to do things like build our dream house (complete with swimming pool) and put all three of our children through college AT THE SAME TIME. I've also had the privilege of working alongside some of the wealthiest women in the country, and, though we were often in competition, they always treated me with warmth and respect as a friend.

So far, I've told you the "fairy tale" part of my story, but, like everyone else, it wasn't always castles and glass slippers. I've had to make several adjustments over the years, like taking time off to help care for aging parents after heart attacks and surgeries, being there when my husband was diagnosed with cancer and required months of treatments, and all the other births, deaths, weddings, joys and sorrows that make up a life. What other company in this world would accept this kind of "job performance?"

With Shirley.

Typically, when production goes down, people are replaced, but then nothing about Mary Kay is typical. When I went to Tennessee to be with my mother after her heart surgery, I was gone for three months, but instead of being asked, "When are you getting back to work?" I got a personal letter from Mary Kay telling me that I was where I should be and that we were in her prayers.

Over the years, I've been asked many times when I'm going to retire. My response is always the same: "If you could win cars, trips, and diamonds, write your own paycheck, and take time off whenever you needed to for your family . . . would you quit??!"

It Takes a Village

> *"There can be no vulnerability without risk;*
> *there can be no community without*
> *vulnerability; there can be no peace,*
> *and ultimately no life, without community."*
> —M. SCOTT PECK

I WAS DEFINITELY NOT IN KANSAS ANYMORE. Or Texas either, for that matter. And even though it wasn't a twister that relocated us nine hundred miles to the east (it was my husband's promotion), I felt every bit as lost as Dorothy on her first day in Oz when we pulled into the driveway of our house in Greenville, South Carolina. This was the "Deep South," and even though Texas is often referred to as "southern," I was now in the bona-fide, below-the-Mason-Dixon, former Confederate South, and I knew I had a lot to learn before I became a part of this new community (if, in fact, that was even possible).

I suppose that if life (or more specifically, Mary Kay) hadn't happened, I would have just continued to socialize with the small circle of friends that had relocated with us from Texas, living in an insulated little community unto ourselves much like my friend and mentor Helen McVoy described when she told me about living in Saudi Arabia where all of the Americans lived in a small, protected area maintained by her husband's company for employees and their families. That was no longer an option, however, when I received the infamous termination letter I described to you earlier and decided I wasn't going down without a fight. If I was going to meet my goal to remain active in the Company, I was going to have to venture out amongst the natives and put some product on the faces of those southern belles.

> When I received the infamous termination letter I . . . decided I wasn't going down without a fight.

A funny thing happened on the way to the mailbox (and the bank) with that termination revoking order, however, something I never would have expected. If you had asked me about the "Mary Kay community" back then, I would have told you that, if such a thing even existed, it was in Dallas. After all, that's where the headquarters, the staff, most of the sales force, and Mary Kay herself were located, so whatever community there was would have to be in Big D, right? Except that as I began to offer the Mary Kay opportunity to my new neighbors in South Carolina, I soon found that these women, mostly housewives with husbands, children, and a full social calendar to tend to, were as restless as I had been back in Texas and were champing at the bit to find an outlet for their energy, intelligence, and creativity that was different from the "traditional" southern role that they, their mothers, and their mothers' mothers had always followed.

Well, little did I realize it at the time, but while we were teaching classes, holding meetings, and swelling our ranks with new recruits anxious to take advantage of this new opportunity working for Mary something-or-other (prior to my arrival there had been no sales force presence in South Carolina so "Mary Who?" was a common question), we were building our own community right there on the eastern front. We soon realized that we had more in common with one another as entrepreneurs and fledgling small business owners than we had differences as Texans and South Carolinians.

The South Carolina Unit, dressed and ready for our first Seminar Awards Night.

We shared goals and business ideas along with victories and hardships. We were each others' sounding boards, cheerleaders, and shoulders to cry on, and together we quickly built the most successful Unit in the country. Oh, and that other community in Dallas? They couldn't wait to bring us west to share what we had learned and continue to build the national community that was growing by leaps and bounds as we helped one another fulfill Mary Kay's dream of improving the lives of women everywhere.

For those of you who may not have spent much time in the "Pink Bubble" (the phrase we use to describe the unique culture of Mary Kay), that word I've been tossing around, "community," may sound a little trite these days. After all, every company, country club, school, and housing division seems to have one and can't wait to tell you about it in their advertising copy, newsletters, and billboards. But in the paraphrased words of Marie Osmond, Mary Kay was community when community wasn't (yet) cool. I'll admit that I'm no expert and can't say exactly what makes a group of people who may have one or more things in common a true community, but, quoting Justice Stewart, "I know it when I see it," and I've always seen it in Mary Kay.

> We were each others' sounding boards, cheerleaders, and shoulders to cry on.

I want to be clear, though, that I'm not suggesting

the members of our community can't stand on their own two feet. The Mary Kay sales force have always been a resilient bunch and are quite capable of pulling themselves up by the bootstraps most of the time. I'll never forget the words of my first line Director Bertha Lindsay, for example, who earned her first Mary Kay car during the three months that elapsed between the death of her mother and father.

Bertha Lindsay

When asked how she managed to keep working during such a trying time, she said: "I realized healing begins when self-pity ends," and that same work ethic served her well as she went on to earn nine pink Cadillacs and appeared in the Queen's Court of Sales twenty-four times, the Queen's Court of Recruiting fifteen times, and Unit Circle twenty-one times (one being Circle of Excellence). Sometimes, however, even the ablest among us need a helping hand, and that's when a strong community can make the difference between a detour and a dead end. But rather than try to describe this elusive concept called "community," I'd like to introduce you to Sherry Williams, who has experienced what it means to be a part of the Mary Kay family more fully than just about anyone I know, and let her inspiring words paint a picture you'll never forget.

Sherry

When I won my first pink Cadillac, I had only been in the company for two years, and then, with those shiny gold keys still jingling in the pocket of my Director's suit, I was also crowned Queen of the Pearl Seminar Queen's Court of Recruiting. Thinking back on that exciting time, it was such a humbling experience to have the privilege of teaching women how to have a successful home-based business and then to be recognized on stage at Seminar and given a trophy on wheels. Today, however, with the benefit of perfect hindsight, I am particularly appreciative of my early successes because God knew that shortly I would have challenges that would not allow me to work toward and achieve such lofty goals.

Not quite a year after that eventful Seminar, I was diagnosed with breast cancer for the first time. I remember being completely taken by surprise because I had no family history, never smoked, and was very physically active, working out and participating in sports whenever I could. Shaken but determined to overcome this unexpected challenge, I underwent a lumpectomy, chemotherapy, and radiation shortly after my diagnosis, trying my best to maintain a positive attitude through it all despite the toll it was taking on my body. Just as I was coming through what I assumed would be the worst of it, however, I received more bad news when, the week before my last chemo treatment, I was diagnosed again in my other breast. It was quite devastating because I was really looking forward to getting my life back.

Though single, I was fortunate not to have to shoulder this burden alone because my Mary Kay family was there for me. It was as if the Army showed up to provide me with help I didn't even know I needed. And help they did because, with the unflagging support of my "army," I managed to rank number thirteen in the Queen's Court of Recruiting despite having to schedule chemo treatments before and after Seminar.

My second round of treatment was far more intense, but, fortunately, so was my support. After I had my bilateral mastectomy with tram flap reconstruction surgery (if you don't know what that is, consider yourself fortunate), the Mary Kay Directors in Chicago went into overdrive. They helped train my consultants, created and distributed my newsletter, sent me to Dallas to meet with Mary Kay's personal physician, cooked and delivered food to me every week, even purchased my Director's suit and then told me not to worry. Naively, I thought it would

Not quite a year after that eventful Seminar, I was diagnosed with breast cancer for the first time.

only be a few weeks after surgery before I was able to start working at a reasonable pace again but, in reality, it took almost a year for me to fully recover. The entire time, however, my Mary Kay family continued to support me, anticipating my every need. They sent me cards, healing prayers, and even CHECKS. I could not believe the outpouring of support from Mary Kay people, not just in Chicago, but all over the country.

This is what I mean when I refer to the Mary Kay community and why I think it is unique in corporate America. Before I started my Mary Kay business, I was a branch manager at a local Chicago bank, and I am sure that my bank co-workers would not have done a fraction of what my Mary Kay family did for me.

Once I had fully recovered, I relocated to the Phoenix area to rebuild my business away from the challenges of harsh Chicago winters. And though I was relieved not to have to worry about an untimely winter storm wiping out a week's worth of appointments or being stranded while waiting to be dug out of the snow, life still happened.

Upon arrival in Phoenix, I tried to hit the ground running; picking up where I left off after my most recent diagnosis and treatment. Though relieved to finally be working consistently again, it was only a year later that I found myself in yet another series of waiting rooms and doctor's offices when my mother was diagnosed with breast cancer. Fortunately, because of my experience, her doctors had been screening her more closely and were able to diagnose her at stage zero, meaning a mass had not yet formed, and she would only need radiation therapy. Though grateful for the optimistic prognosis, I once again had to scale back my business as I flew

I found myself in yet another series of waiting rooms and doctor's offices.

back and forth to Atlanta to support my mother during her treatments. Fortunately, my mother made a full recovery, but there were still challenges waiting down the road.

Though I have been cancer-free for almost ten years now, I had to endure two more recurrences, along with the attendant radiation and chemotherapy regimens, before I could finally declare myself "in remission." In addition, I have had thyroid (thankfully benign), hernia, and two knee surgeries to contend with, all the while adjusting the pace of my Mary Kay business to the challenges of the moment. Of course, with all the support that's been given to me, I am quick to "pay it forward," and for a while was spending one week out of every month in Chicago taking care of my great-aunt, who was suffering from dementia. That's just how flexible this business can be.

With Sherry at Awards Night.

In addition to the support of the sales force during those difficult times, I received a helping hand from the Company when they started the Customer Delivery Service (CDS). Thanks to CDS, I was better able to service my customers when I was sick or had to travel because I could have their orders shipped directly from the Company and didn't have to maintain high levels of inventory when I had to work my business on a part-time basis. This kind of "in-house" support from corporate goes hand-in-hand with the personal support I was receiving from my fellow sales force members and is completely consistent with Mary Kay's commitment to creating a wholistic community that could provide for its members when they hit life's inevitable speed bumps, allowing us to continue to work our business with, in the immortal words of the Beatles, "a little help from [our] friends."

When asked why I am still with Mary Kay despite all the ups, downs, and sudden stops, having to watch my peers qualify as Nationals as I was undergoing yet another round of cancer treatments, it is because I love this Mary Kay business so much. Though I was able to make a subsequent appearance in the Queen's Court of Recruiting, achieve Unit Circle three times, and earn a career-high monthly commission check over $8,900, what I treasure most is the support I have received from my Director girlfriends and the entire Mary Kay community. I

> **This kind of "in-house" support from corporate . . . is completely consistent with Mary Kay's commitment to create a wholistic community.**

truly believe their embodiment of Mary Kay's God first, family second, and career third philosophy is the reason why, despite all of my health and life challenges, I will always be a part of this amazing company. It is rare to find a career that you truly love but I am still as excited about all of the women I can help through Mary Kay's products and philosophy as I was when I started eighteen years ago.

Who's Got Your Back?

*"Husbands and wives generally understand
when opposition will be in vain."*

—JANE AUSTEN

I WAS SHIFTING INTO HIGH GEAR and headed for the fast lane. One look at the terrified expression on my husband's face, however, convinced me to pull over and let him back in the driver's seat for the remainder of the test drive. I was about to make what I considered a critical investment in my future by spending the largest monthly commission check I had earned to date on a new sports car I knew my husband, Bruce, had been eyeing for months. With the stroke of a pen (in my

Devin and Bruce, with the car I bought
for him with just one Mary Kay check.

checkbook), I was painting one of those pictures worth a thousand words to show how mutually beneficial my Mary Kay business could be if he would stay on board while I worked to realize what I now knew was my true potential.

Mary Kay taught us from day one that our families could either be our biggest obstacles or our biggest supporters, and therefore learning how to get, and keep, them in our corner was one of the most important skills we could acquire (and teach). Many women

Joanne Fogle

today believe concepts like "Husbands' Classes" at Seminar and the "Covered Dish Suppers" my Unit used to put on where we fed the husbands and then let them see the prizes and recognition their wives (or more important the other husbands' wives) were receiving to get them "on board" are outdated and a relic of the pre-feminist era. Perhaps, but anyone who has ever had the privilege of attending one of Joe and Joanne Fogle's famous steak dinners, which Bruce and I attended every chance we got, knows the power of a good meal and good company when you're trying to rally support for your team (and given that Joanne debuted as a Director over forty years ago and has multiple Cadillacs, Queen's Courts of Sales, and Queen's Courts of

Recruiting under her belt, she must be doing something right). So, while such tactics may seem obsolete to the truly liberated, I would argue that for most women in the world today, winning the support of a spouse, significant other, or dependent family member is every bit as critical as it was for those of us who had to manage traditional stereotypes back in the day.

Ironically, one of the reasons women in Mary Kay had to address the "husband issue" in the early years of the Company was because ours was the only career opportunity flexible enough to even get a toehold in a traditional nuclear family. If we had headed for the door, briefcase in hand, announcing that we were embarking on a "career" and might not be home for supper, we wouldn't have made it very far before our spouses, family, and even friends put us back in our place. Armed with a beauty case and our own business, however, a new Mary Kay Consultant could stay home, take care of the children, and still have supper ready most of the time if we could just get a hall pass for our Unit meetings, classes, and, once a year, Seminar.

> Armed with a beauty case and our own business, . . . a new Mary Kay Consultant could stay home.

"But things are different now," I hear today's young women protest, and, in many ways, they are. Most women entering the workforce today assume that their significant others will support them in their career, and they are usually right. Unfortunately, that "nuclear" family (i.e., husband, wife, and 2.5 children) is becoming less and less the norm as economic and social factors force the modern woman to adapt to constantly changing configurations that redefine the concept of "family." Aging parents, siblings with health or job issues, un- or underemployed adult children (often from one or both spouse's previous marriages), dren (often from one or both spouse's previous marriages), and, of course, that husband and 2.5 biological children may all be living under the same roof at one time or another and looking to the wife/mother/sister/ daughter for emotional and financial support.

> The new Consultant . . . may find the door blocked by those that . . . need to be fed, bathed, changed, consoled, and funded.

While the various demands inherent in sharing one's home with all of these family members/cohabitants makes a strong case for a career with the flexibility of Mary Kay that encourages women to put God first, family second, and career third, it also requires a bit of strategy. The new Consultant heading out to teach a skin care class may find the door blocked by those that feel they need to be fed, bathed, changed, consoled, and funded before their primary caregiver is allowed to leave. In this situation, all of those techniques we developed in the good old days when all we had to manage was one simple husband (no offense to *manus domesticus*) can come in quite handy.

I am also acutely aware that many women in developing countries, and even in ethnic enclaves around the U.S., are still very much limited by the traditions and expectations of their culture. For these women, any career opportunity that does not allow them to fulfill their traditional role in the family and in the community is a non-starter. In these circumstances, a value system of God first, family second, and career third is not optional, it is a way of life that must be adhered to if a woman is to pursue any opportunity at all.

The good news is that the technique to be deployed is fairly simple and one that Mary Kay taught us from day one: What's In It For Me, or WIIFM. In my case, or rather in my husband's case, it was a new sports car. For the husband of another Unit member during those critical days when we were making our way to Number One in the country, it was a golf membership. Whatever the means, the message was the same: help me help you by achieving our goals together. I remember Mary Kay always encouraged us to study the home environment of the women we were trying to develop as Consultants and Directors to find out what they and their families were

> In these circumstances, a value system of God first, family second, and career third is . . . a way of life.

passionate about. In one case, a budding Director was at wit's end and on the verge of quitting because her daughter wouldn't stop crying every time her mother left the house to go to a class or Unit meeting. Knowing her daughter's passion was horses (not hard to figure out once I had been in her house, which was filled with every kind of horse memorabilia), I proposed that every time Mom needed to go out, she would deposit five dollars into a "horse fund" if the daughter would support her by not crying when she left the house. Sure enough, it wasn't long before I had a new Director and the little girl had a new horse.

Of course, sometimes that significant other we think will have to be slowly and strategically coaxed into supporting us ends up jumping on board with both feet when "life happens," as it did with former Dingler Area Director Robbie Foley.

Robbie

It had been fourteen years since I resigned from my first attempt at a Mary Kay business, but after meeting and talking to National Sales Director Doretha Dingler, I was "inspired" to try again. You see, Doretha is not a person, she is a force of nature and by far the most energetic, dynamic, positive, and no-nonsense individual I have ever known. She also has a vocabulary deficiency in that she does not understand the words "impossible," "can't," "quit," or "it won't work." So, knowing I was fighting a losing battle trying to tell her "no," I signed my agreement while the moving truck was literally in the driveway because my family was being relocated from Dallas to Phoenix for my husband Tom's new business. Little did I know Doretha would follow me to Phoenix, whip in hand!

> I signed my agreement while the moving truck was literally in the driveway.

Fast forward several months, and two important events were occurring in my Mary Kay career: 1) I earned my very first Career Car; and 2) I was preparing to submit my Director in Qualification or DIQ card (this is a card we were required to send to the Company informing them of our intention to become a Mary Kay Independent Sales Director). I was charged up and ready to go forward with this wonderful career I had managed to revive, thanks to Doretha's leadership, when my husband Tom came home with some career news of his own.

He walked in a little after five in the afternoon and asked whose red Pontiac Firenza was parked in our driveway. When I proudly announced it was my new Mary Kay car, he was totally shocked because, up to that point, he thought I had just been playing around with make-up. Then he made his two announcements: 1) his business had gone bankrupt; and 2) our house was in foreclosure and we had to be out in thirty days. Tom said he had kept me out of the loop to avoid worrying me until he was absolutely sure how things would turn out. Obviously, they hadn't turned out the way he had hoped.

Little did I realize that my actual Mary Kay career began that very minute. From having a fun little hobby to play with, I had suddenly become the breadwinner of our family until my husband could figure out his next move, and I wasn't at all sure I could pull it off. The panic I had felt the first time I handed out business cards for facial contacts was nothing compared to the breathless, throat-closing, heart-pounding, incapacitating, jelly-kneed reaction I was experiencing at that moment! It's one thing to enjoy the applause and accolades from your Mary Kay peers for having a $500 week in sales, but quite another to need that $500, and a lot more, to support a family of five, a house payment, utilities, food, and tuition for three children in private school.

> I had suddenly become the breadwinner of our family.

Our family considered the options as we tried to come to grips with this incredible change in circumstances. First and foremost, we had to have a place to live, so Tom agreed to locate a rental house that we could move into right away. The second, and to me the most important, decision was whether I should get a "Real Job" or continue to work toward becoming a Mary Kay Director. To my everlasting gratitude, with his world crumbling around him, my husband told me he knew I could do it and that he would handle the move, the kids, and any legal matters necessary to free me up so I could become a Director.

Except for a few mini nervous breakdowns (all mine), things worked out pretty well. I remember one incident though when I was parked in a grocery store parking lot sobbing on my cell phone to Doretha that I was finished, used up, and just couldn't do it anymore. Well, she let me have my pity party and then told me to stop feeling sorry for myself, at which point I threw the phone down on the passenger-side floorboard. I'm not sure what I was hoping for exactly, unless it was that she might think I had left the car? I can still hear her voice to this day from the floorboard: "Robbie, you pick up this phone right now! I know you're still there!" As you might imagine, I picked up the phone, listened to Doretha, and then put the car, and myself, back in gear.

Robbie weighing her options.

Well, I am happy to report that I qualified as a Director and christened my new Unit "Robbie's Redcoats" with the motto "A red coat in every closet and a red car in every garage." Actually, as a result of the Redcoats hard work and dedication (we've made five appearances in Unit Circle), I've had the privilege of parking two pink Cadillacs in my garage as well as accumulating numerous other accolades. Of course, I never could have done it without my family's unflagging support because, whether we bring our families on board gradually or, as in my case, life just throws them over the gunwales, that's when we are truly free to shift into high gear, step on the gas, and get in the fast lane to our dreams.

Strategizing with Robbie in my Dallas office.

The Global Revelation

"The real voyage of discovery consists not in seeking new landscapes, but in having new eyes."
MARCEL PROUST

"FREEZE!" THE MAN SHOUTED, but I kept running. Kept running until I could no longer hear him yelling at me in Italian because his voice had been cut off by the guillotine-like steel contraptions that kept slamming down just behind me as I sprinted down the corridor. Fortunately, this terrifying experience turned out to be nothing more than a fire drill aboard the *Stella Solaris* (the cruise ship we were taking to Israel via the Greek Isles for our annual Top Ten trip with Mary Kay) but, in light of events that had transpired earlier that day (and given that I was certain one of those steel "doors" could have killed me had I been one second slower clearing each portal), my nerves were on edge to say the least.

With Bruce on our eventful cruise aboard the *Stella Solaris.*

Our cruise had been positively uneventful until the moment the Captain gathered us all together to announce that the *Achille Lauro,* an Italian cruise ship sailing in nearby waters, had been hijacked by the Palestine Liberation Organization, and therefore we would be diverting immediately to the nearest secure harbor in Port Said, Egypt. I remember several of us conferred after the briefing and collectively decided we needed to get home as soon as possible. We planned to let Mary Kay Ash know our wishes to abandon the ship immediately, but, before we could go to her, Mary Kay came to us. She announced that the staff had already arranged transportation in small planes that would get us to Athens, Greece, where any of us who wished to get out fast could fly home. The next words out of her mouth, however, stunned everyone: "We will continue this trip for those who wish to remain. I will be staying on the ship." There was a moment of stunned silence after this announcement and then, following the example of "our" captain, everyone agreed to remain aboard. If Mary Kay was going to stay the course, we were going with her.

We knew we were not out of danger yet, however, and were unsure what would happen next, especially in light of the fact that in the context of these anti-American acts of terror we were sailing with a legendary American icon. As you might imagine, it was a sleepless night for most of us, but, when the next day finally dawned, we found ourselves safely docked in

With Mary Kay and the Captain aboard the *Stella Solaris* after our hijacking scare.

Port Said, Egypt. Though we all breathed an enormous sigh of relief, the reality of what had just happened hit home when we looked outside our windows and saw the *Achille Lauro,* whose fifty-two-hour ordeal had ended when the hijackers finally surrendered, docked in the adjacent slip. Though we would never know just how close we came to sharing the fate of the *Achille Lauro* passengers during that harrowing experience, what we did know for certain was that our founder's bravery and leadership were beyond question and that we would never again take our freedom for granted. Our hearts went out to the four hundred and thirty-eight former hostages whose harrowing experience, including the brutal murder of a wheelchair-bound American passenger, was eventually made into a movie, *The Hijacking of the Achille Lauro.*

Once the crisis ended, we resumed an only slightly altered itinerary as we followed Mary Kay's example and soldiered on, determined not to let the terrorists send us scurrying back home. Little did we know then, however, that Mary Kay would soon be doing more than traveling to foreign countries; she would be exporting the Mary Kay opportunity around the world. For many of us in the original Top Ten, these

> Those early trips with Mary Kay and the Top Ten National Sales Directors will always be among the greatest memories of my life.

trips were our first experience traveling internationally, and what an experience it was. Over the years, we would travel to almost every continent and visit cities as diverse as Paris, France, and Hong Kong, China. Being immersed in these different cultures, if only for a few days, gave us a taste (literally) of what it would be like to be surrounded by people with whom you couldn't communicate, didn't understand their traditions (e.g., do you shake hands or kiss them on the cheek?), or even know what to eat (that's a fried what???).

> For many of us . . ., these trips were our first experience traveling internationally.

After each of these Top Ten adventures, we returned to the States with a better appreciation of how lucky we were to be so at home in a society that allowed us to take advantage of opportunities like Mary Kay. We also had greater empathy for those who had immigrated to the U.S. to build a better life for themselves and their families but were struggling to learn our language, laws, and social customs at the same time they were working to grow a Mary Kay business. In fact, I was fortunate enough to have a front-row seat to the personal and professional development of just such a woman. The amazing and flamboyant (I don't think I've ever seen her when she wasn't wearing one of her signature flamboyant hats) Gloria Heyaime.

Gloria

I came from a small town in my native Dominican Republic, and felt I had already done quite well for myself by the time I immigrated to the United States at the tender age of twenty-one. I had a business degree and was married to a physician at the time, but we both had to "revalidate" our degrees in the U.S., and so we moved in with my in-laws in Tampa, Florida, while we completed our studies. At least that was the plan. Little did I know that my newly minted business degree was going to be put to good use sooner rather than later when I joined Mary Kay after only being in this country for TWO DAYS. I didn't speak English or even know how to drive, and, worse, I was so shy and introverted I didn't know anyone except "the in-laws." So, given all of that you might ask, how did I learn about Mary Kay?

Well, a few months earlier while visiting family in the U.S. on Christmas vacation, a lovely lady named Betsy Walker stopped me in a mall and started talking. When I didn't respond, she simply turned to the person I was with and continued the conversation until, eventually, they exchanged phone numbers, with me still wondering what in the world was going on. After Betsy left, my friend told me "She is a Mary Kay Consultant and thought you could be good for this business. When I told her you didn't speak English and were very shy, she said 'Great! We need Spanish-speaking consultants in this area, and don't worry about shyness because we have an extensive training program that will increase self-esteem and self-confidence.'" Okay I thought, from here to Hollywood!

When I returned to the States two months later, this time for good, I hadn't forgotten about Mary Kay and decided I was willing to take a chance on this company that offered extensive training and unlimited opportunity. We arrived on a Saturday, and by Monday I was a Mary Kay Beauty Consultant. Of course, I had no idea what that meant except that they teach you everything you need to know, and, if you follow it step by step, a whole new world opens up! Fortunately, my in-laws were willing to take turns driving AND translating for me twice a week (for an entire year!) so I could learn to look people in the eye, stop crying, and not shake so much when I had to speak to someone (I was later diagnosed with extreme social anxiety, but I never told anyone about it until 2009 when it became increasingly difficult for me to go to events without having a panic attack). Thanks to the Mary Kay training that helped me increase my confidence and overcome my fears, however, I was soon off and running with a new career.

Okay I thought, from here to Hollywood!

I finished my Perfect Start, became a Star consultant, and DIDN'T FAINT! On the contrary, I found out there was another person living inside of me, one that loved to teach and who wanted a life free of schedules, traffic jams, and limited income! Fears be darned! I decided all of the fun, prizes, cash, and dressing up was worth learning to manage those "ghosts" that were keeping me a prisoner inside my own head.

I eventually decided I wanted to grow up to become a National Sales Director one day, I then found out that my National, Doretha Dingler, was not only the Number One NSD in my Seminar, but was also a Senior National because she had already groomed several NSDs from the Dingler Area. She also seemed kind of shy despite her success so I knew I was definitely where I needed to be. I wanted to become one of those women Mary Kay described as "ordinary but with extra-ordinary determination," someone "who will help make the position of Directorship so esteemed that one day little girls around the world, when asked what they want to be when they grow up, will proudly say 'a Mary Kay Director.'"

> I . . . was told to "put my affairs in order."

Unfortunately, learning English and overcoming shyness weren't the only challenges I had to face. I spent a month at the M.D. Anderson Cancer Center in Houston after receiving a terminal diagnosis and was told to "put my affairs in order" because in six months, the cancer would be too big to contain. Well, it apparently wasn't too big for God to contain because I went into remission "in the nick of time" according to my doctors, and I can't tell you what a relief it is to experience such a miracle. While I had been living under that dark cloud, however, I also had to keep up my Mary Kay business because at that point in my life, I had no spouse, no alimony, no inheritance, and no other job. So what did I have? My faith, my few dearest friends, and my Mary Kay. Apparently, that was enough. I even received a call from Mary Kay herself offering her prayers and support because she had heard about my situation from Doretha. Fortunately, I wasn't home at the time, so I was able to save the message. Thank goodness for friends in high places.

Though I could easily have thrown a good old-fashioned "pity party" after going through such an ordeal, my life was filled instead with gratitude and joy because I knew that if I lived to be a hundred, it would never be long enough to thank Mary Kay properly. And what, you may ask, do I have to be thankful for? Six pink Cadillacs, twelve appearances in Unit Circle (one of those being Circle of Excellence), commission checks in excess of $10,000, and all the cash and prizes that go along with reaching that

Gloria, confident and relaxed in America.

level of accomplishment. What I am most grateful for, however, are the amazing women who have been put in my path,
whose lives (and the lives of their families) are now changed
for the better because they were willing to put their trust in
me. I am also proud to report that many of these women are
now building their own National areas as they continue to
become the best version of themselves, and that goes on
whether I am here or not!

My goal is to be a National Sales Director in the very near
future and, armed with determination and a positive attitude,
I know that I can. In this amazing company, I have found my
voice, my passion, my mission, and my ministry. As cheesy as
it sounds, I also found the meaning of my name. You see, my
maiden name, Gloria Celeste, loosely translated means "glory
from the heavens," and that is exactly what I have received
from Mary Kay.

Fire Me!

"It is not the mountain we conquer,
but ourselves."

—EDMUND HILLARY

I WAS IN THE WRONG CAR. Oh sure, it was my key that opened the door and started the ignition to a brand new pink Cadillac, but this was definitely not my car. My car was the more expensive, more sophisticated pink Cadillac being driven by

Receiving the keys to my first pink Cadillac.

National Sales Directors like my friend and mentor Helen McVoy. By all accounts, I had been very successful as a Director and should have been more than satisfied with my Number One status, and a free Cadillac to boot, but the day I saw that Helen was driving a BETTER pink Cadillac, I knew I was in the wrong car. I immediately called Mary Kay headquarters to find out what I had to do get one just like it

I was on target for National—whether the Company knew it or not.

and was politely but firmly informed that those cars were reserved for Nationals only. Well, by the time I hung up the phone, my competitive streak had turned a bright green, and I was on target for National—whether the Company knew it or not.

I will admit that I've always been competitive. Whether it was a footrace with my cousins at family gatherings, checkers with my father's friends at my uncle's barbershop (because he bet them they couldn't beat me—and he was right), or math contests with my teachers at school (here's a hint for any students out there—don't beat your teacher), I was always up for a challenge. Looking back over my career with perfect hindsight, I can see that it was that same drive to win that fueled my achievements in Mary Kay. Once I set a goal, I was like a runner hearing the starting gun at a track meet who is determined to break that tape and be first across the finish line. So, laced up and poised at the starting blocks, I was ready to make my run at NSD and had an incredible Unit that was as excited as I was at the prospect of becoming the Dingler Area.

We've heard many stories in this book about those who could not or chose not to pursue Director or National status and they have shown us how Mary Kay can meet anyone where she is at any given time or situation in life. For those with the drive and the opportunity, however, Mary Kay also offers a fast lane. It's all the way to the left and not for the faint of heart, but if you, like former Dingler Area Director Tina Dees, are suited up with your seatbelt fastened when opportunity knocks, you're in for the ride of your life.

Tina

I had been coasting along perfectly content, working my Mary Kay business part-time as I focused on my full-time job, a second job on the weekends, and going to school at night. Even as I was working my way up the corporate ladder, however, I always knew that some day Mary Kay would be my one and only dream career, and promised myself that no one would ever take that away from me. I watched a Seminar video every morning to stay inspired, fascinated by the Cinderella stories and "wowed" by the beauty, glitz, and glamour that I knew I would experience one day when I was finally able to attend a Seminar.

I was more than maintaining the status quo, however. Though painfully shy and terrified of public speaking (I dropped the same Speech class three times in college), I was able to take advantage of the new Consultant training to help build my confidence, and then, after carefully following the instructions of my Director, I managed to earn the use of my first Mary Kay car in only five months. Step by step and one face at a time, I grew as a person and as a Consultant. I learned the power of goal setting and that if

> My commitment to Mary Kay was put to the test when I was called into my boss's office and given an ultimatum.

I wasn't setting the next goal and stepping out of my comfort zone, I would soon be "stuck in a rut" and stop growing. Eventually, still working part-time, I qualified as a Director, but then, three months later, my commitment to Mary Kay was put to the test when I was called into my boss's office and given an ultimatum.

He said, and I quote, "I know you did that little Mary Kay thing when I hired you, but I need you to quit that now because I'm transferring you to another office, and it's against company policy." My response? No way! They were not going to steal my dream. I knew there was no other place in the world that offered Mary Kay's flexibility, unlimited opportunity (i.e., no "glass ceiling"), freedom to put my faith and family ahead of my career, and the opportunity to run as fast (or as slow) as I chose. I had also gotten to know many very successful women in Mary Kay, and I realized that the only person standing between me and the level of success they had achieved was the woman I saw in the mirror every day. I'm sure my boss was stunned that I refused such a "career opportunity," but I knew my Mary Kay business was waiting for me, and I wasn't going to waste another moment!

What an amazing turning point in my life. I knew the time had come to run in faith and never look back. Only eighteen months after signing my Consultant agreement, I flew (for the first time) to Dallas for Sales Director training and had the honor of not only meeting but actually receiving my

Tina enjoying life in the "Fast Lane" (and Monte Carlo!).

training directly from Mary Kay herself. Well, I guess she must have gotten through to me because I went on to become a Top Director nationwide, qualify for Unit Circle thirteen times (three of those being Circle of Excellence), earn six pink Cadillacs, cash checks in excess of $13,000, and win four Top Director trips to destinations as exotic as Monte Carlo and the Greek Isles. From that scared, insecure little girl from South Georgia, I have managed to grow into the confident, secure woman that I believe God always intended me to be. Best of all, I have the privilege of going out and making that same kind of difference for other women who, just like me, were only waiting for someone to teach them how to dream.

Hollywood or Bust

*"You have to go through the falling down
in order to learn to walk."*
—CAROL BURNETT

"I NEED SEVENTEEN THOUSAND DOLLARS. CASH," said the man in broken English and Arabic. Locked inside a closed jewelry store with two strange men who apparently had never heard of American Express, I had no idea how I was going to get out of this. Fortunately, I was with my friend and fellow Top Ten National Helen McVoy, whose inclination toward adventurous shopping sprees had gotten us into this fine mess to begin with as far as I was concerned. True to form, Helen looked the man straight in the eye and without skipping a beat said, "I'll get it from the Captain."

The next thing I knew we were in the back seat of a Mercedes being driven through Port Said, Egypt, by the shop owner and our "guide" (we wrongly assumed he had been hired by Mary Kay travel when he appeared alongside us earlier that day and explained that he would take us anywhere we wished to go) riding shotgun as we made our way back to port where our cruise ship was docked. By the time we arrived at the security checkpoint, I was deep in silent prayer offering God a lifetime of penance if we could just make it safely back on board. Helen, however, never broke stride as she made a beeline for the Captain and informed him, as if this happened every day, that we needed $17,000 cash to pay for the jewelry "we" had just purchased from a local merchant.

Though a novel experience for Helen, she was politely but firmly told, "no," the Captain didn't carry that kind of cash on board and, while he was at it, "no," we shouldn't be riding around Port Said in private cars with men we didn't know while carrying expensive jewelry. Point taken. But then, just when I thought

this little drama had finally come to a merciful end, I was somehow elected to be the bearer of bad news to two soon-

Shopping with Helen McVoy in Port Said, Egypt.

to-be-very-angry men waiting for us at the docks. Once again I felt a familiar knot forming in my stomach when, in a flash of inspiration, I came up with a solution. I ran to the railing on the port side of the ship, waved my arms to get the attention of our two new best friends who where anxiously awaiting our return down below, cupped my hands around my mouth, and shouted, "We can't get the money!" Having no desire to stick around for their reaction to this unwelcome news, I turned and headed for my cabin where I planned to have a well-deserved nervous breakdown.

> I planned to have a well-deserved nervous breakdown.

Though it makes a funny story these days, that experience illustrates why choosing the right friend and mentor was an important part of learning to overcome those fears and insecurities that dogged me early in my career. Observing Helen's indomitable spirit firsthand and watching her tackle obstacles with a "find-a-way or make-a-way" attitude taught me what was possible when a woman fully owned who she was and what she could accomplish. I like to think that I ultimately met and exceeded the high bar that Mary Kay set for us when she created the leadership position of National Sales Director, and that I, in turn, have helped others achieve their goals. After all, that's the way our community works, by passing on that which is given to us and teaching as we were taught until we are all standing arm in arm on stage together celebrating one another's success. Simply put, as long-time Dingler Area member June Hockenberry can attest, it's important who your friends are.

June

My story really begins one cold, mid-winter day in Michigan when my father, who had been first trumpet for the Detroit Symphony for as long as I could remember, called from California to announce that we were, literally, "going to Hollywood." I suppose this shouldn't have been a complete surprise since

he had actually been working in Tinseltown ever since receiving an invitation to help record soundtracks for the Hollywood film industry. He must have decided the California weather agreed with him because one day he made it a permanent gig, bought a house, and sent for his frozen family back in Michigan. He didn't have to ask twice.

I was twelve years old when we arrived in the City of Angels, and Hollywood was in its heyday. I must have seen every movie star of that era, most often at the Lux Radio Theater, where anyone could sit in the audience and watch reenactments of current movies, usually featuring the actual star him or herself. I remember my best friend's grandmother styled Lucille Ball's hair so we got to see her quite a bit. My first celebrity sighting "in the wild," however, was Doris Day. She was crossing Hollywood Boulevard at, you guessed it, Vine Street (which was just about five blocks from our new house), and I was too awestruck to ask for an autograph.

My second sighting was slightly more successful. I saw a man walking out of a saddle store, and, when I looked down, there was Alan Ladd (even at age twelve I was quite a bit taller than he was). Although Ladd was a huge star at the time, he was so nice and down-to-earth that he even went back into the saddle store to ask the owner for pencil and paper so he could give me his autograph. Unfortunately, my brother fared much worse than I did in the autograph department. His most notable encounter with celebrity was when Humphrey Bogart pulled into the gas station where he worked, jumped out of his car, and asked, "Where is it?" Star-struck and dumbfounded, my brother couldn't for the life of him figure out what "it" was until Bogey finally spotted the restroom on his own and dashed off to avail himself of the facilities. Afterward, he simply hopped back in his car and sped away, leaving my brother empty-handed (except for the gas pump, of course).

My Hollywood High School classmate, Carol Burnett, became a comedic actress and much beloved celebrity.

I suppose you could say my fifteen minutes of fame came years later when my Hollywood High School classmate, Carol

Burnett, became a successful comedic actress and much beloved celebrity. When we were in school, she was just one of the girls. Not the class clown or the "cool kid" destined to be most popular, just a regular Joe (or Josephine). Of course, later she would be the hit of our class reunions. I remember

one year when they were having a roll call for each class year, Carol said to me, "Let's do the Tarzan yell," so I passed the word along, and when our year came up we all belted out the classic Carol Burnett Tarzan yell before breaking up into uncontrollable laughter.

June with friend and former classmate Carol Burnett.

Despite being surrounded by famous people who seemed to be as comfortable with an autograph seeker or schoolmate as being in front of an audience, I was always painfully shy. Like most girls, I had my fair share of crushes in high school, but only remember going out on one date. To make things worse, when I went off to college at UCLA I tried to break out of my shell by pledging a sorority, but, instead of becoming an outgoing sorority girl as I had planned, I compounded my self-conscious shyness by becoming extremely sarcastic. Honestly, I don't know how anyone put up with me during that time.

My real personal growth didn't begin until I was well into my career with Lockheed Missiles and Space Company and my friend and co-worker Luci Logan came to my desk to tell me about this exciting new business she was starting as a Consultant for Mary Kay Cosmetics. Even though she had only been a Consultant for one week, she told me everything she knew about the company (which wasn't much), but what she lacked in knowledge, she made up for in enthusiasm. I told her that Mary Kay sounded perfect for her but that I could never do something like that. I couldn't stop thinking about everything she had told me, however, and most of all how excited she was.

I remember this was a Friday, and I found myself thinking, *I'm almost forty years old, and I don't even know how to wear eye shadow. Maybe Mary Kay could teach me how to do that and help me build my confidence as well.* I finally worked up the courage to call Luci later that evening and tell her, "I'll do it. I want to do what you do."

"Well," she said. "I don't know if the company is still hiring so you'll have to wait until Monday." Now I really wanted to be a Consultant but I had to wait through the longest weekend of my life to find out if I was going to be "hired." Well, when Monday finally rolled around I was informed that I was in luck, the opportunity was still available, so I signed up right away with a Star Consultant order and joined the soon-to-be Unit of Director in Qualification Carolyn Antle. When Carolyn debuted as a Director at Seminar that year wearing a beautiful royal blue suit with white piping and matching hat, I remember thinking, "I want that suit!"

> **I'm almost forty years old, and I don't even know how to wear eye shadow.**

Even though it would take nine years before I committed to becoming a Director, that Seminar marked the beginning of an era of personal growth that would see the old shy, self-conscious, sarcastic me eventually fade into oblivion. I remember having to leave early to catch my flight back to California, so I took a cab to the airport by myself and had a coffee and a piece of pie at the airport coffee shop while I waited for my plane to begin boarding. Now, for most people this would be a completely unremarkable event, but I had been driving from the San Francisco Bay area (where I now lived) to Hollywood almost every week and eating candy bars from gas stations just so I wouldn't have to go into a diner and actually talk to someone. I was definitely tired of candy bars. And being afraid.

When I finally did get around to becoming a Director, I liked it so much, I did it twice!

What I had learned from Mary Kay herself, as well as from the Directors whose classes I had attended, was that I was worth something. I was important, and, best of all, I could make a difference in the lives of other women. I think sitting there in that coffee shop, eating that piece of pie like I owned the place and feeling good about myself and my future, was one of the proudest moments of my life.

When I finally did get around to becoming a Director, I liked it so much, I did it twice! I admit the first time was probably just to see if those Director's checks I was always reading about in *Applause* were real. They were. In fact, I saved the tax return from my first year as a Director that showed I had "given myself a raise" of $29,000, quite a tidy sum at the time. My goal had always been to retire at fifty-five, however, so when I hit double nickels, I did just that and hung up my Director's suit. Or so I thought. The very next year the Director's suit was a beautiful electric blue, and I knew I had to have it (are you seeing a pattern here?). So, I re-upped as they say in the Army, posted fifteen color copies of the promotional brochure with that seductive suit in my office for inspiration, and re-debuted as a Director four months later.

I can't think of a word powerful enough to adequately describe what Directorship meant to me. Yes, I had the privilege of appearing in the Queen's Court of Sales and qualifying for Unit Circle, as well as earning cars and various other accolades, but, even without those accomplishments, the Mary Kay training I received has made such a difference in my life that I would not have missed it for anything. I went from being too shy to walk into a coffee shop to being asked to teach classes on warm chatter. Later in my Mary Kay career, I used to joke that if I

June riding high with her new career.

saw a woman driving down the street, I would run the car down to tell the driver I wanted to talk to her about Mary Kay. I became so confident in fact that I started marketing myself as a motivational speaker. The first time I was asked, I really didn't want to do it so I told the person my fee was $500, a figure so outlandish I assumed no one would ever hire me. To my complete amazement, they agreed, and I that's how I learned there was one more thing I could do if I only believed in myself enough to take the chance, just like Mary Kay taught me.

When my husband retired from his own job several years ago, I finally resigned my Directorship once and for all and joined him in "retiring" to Consultant status. That may seem like an odd way to spend one's golden years, but I still love this business and it continues to thrive, even during tough times. My Mary Kay business always reminded me of my favorite poem, "'Hope' is the thing with feathers," by Emily Dickinson:

> *"Hope" is the thing with feathers—*
> *That perches in the soul—*
> *And sings the tune without the words—*
> *And never stops—at all—*
>
> *And sweetest—in the Gale—is heard—*
> *And sore must be the storm—*
> *That could abash the little Bird*
> *That kept so many warm—*
>
> *I've heard it in the chillest land—*
> *And on the strangest Sea—*
> *Yet—never—in Extremity,*
> *It asked a crumb—of me.*

How to Get to Carnegie Hall

"Every child is an artist. The problem is how to remain an artist once [she] grows up."
—Pablo Picasso

THE AUDIENCE ERUPTED IN THUNDEROUS APPLAUSE as they jumped to their feet for a standing ovation following my brilliant performance at Carnegie Hall. As I was taking my bows and considering what to play for an encore, however, I heard a small but familiar voice coming from stage left. "Dee Dee? Dee Dee, was that you?" Coming out of my daydream, I realized I was still in my living room at our new house in Dallas, and it was my granddaughter, Brittany, who had been calling me.

I had been trying out the piano left by the previous owners, and it hadn't occurred to me that Brittany had never heard me play. Truthfully, I felt a little rusty as I worked my way through the limited repertoire of songs

I knew by heart, but Brittany thought someone had turned up the stereo to play some jazz music at full blast. I laughed as I explained to her that I used to play quite a bit growing up (I even have a picture of myself in formal attire playing "Down in The Valley" at my first piano recital), but these days I didn't have much opportunity and had forgotten how much I enjoyed it. In fact, in my wanderings down memory lane gathering material for my first book *In Pink,* I came across a letter from Hellen Brookshire, one of my first Offspring Directors in Greenville, South Carolina, sent in honor of the Dingler Area's twenty-fifth anniversary, that reminded me of some "professional" piano playing I had also forgotten about. She wrote: "I will always remember walking into our Greenville sales meetings while you played the piano with your wig on crooked."

Well, I'm quite sure she was mistaken on that second point, but I do remember having a lot of fun playing "I've Got That Mary Kay Enthusiasm" and

My ticket to Carnegie Hall (with my photo in the background).

"Nothing Could Be Finer Than to Be in Carolina" as we warmed up the crowd.

I'm happy to report that I've reconnected with my music in recent years (but don't look for me on the Carnegie Hall marquee anytime soon), and I find having that outlet for creative expression very therapeutic.

Though I have never considered myself an artist by any means, I can appreciate the passion of those who do, and I have always enjoyed being around creative and talented women such as former Dingler Area Director Betsy Baker, who remembers her early days in Mary Kay with a uniquely artistic slant:

Betsy weaving her magic at Awards Night.

"As an artist, a potter, and a weaver, I can recall the pleasure I felt as I learned to make the clay or the fibers do what I wanted, but then, when I began my Mary Kay career, I quickly realized it wasn't going to be that way with people. Through my training, however, I learned that I could do something better. I could help mold other women into who THEY wanted to be."

Betsy also learned that "starving" and "artist" don't have to be synonymous, thanks to her sixteen appearances (and counting) in the Queen's Court of Sales, five Mary Kay cars, and numerous other accolades. Fortunately, Mary Kay is filled with creative people because it is one of the few career opportunities that allows a woman to earn a decent living while still having time to develop as an artist. In fact, survey the attendees at any Seminar gathering and you're likely to find musicians, painters, potters, and artists of all stripes pursuing their muse and a pink Cadillac at the same time.

> Mary Kay is well positioned for its next fifty years because our village is growing rapidly.

I believe this diversity of backgrounds, talents, and ability is one of the things that makes the Mary Kay community so rich. If, as is so often said these days, "It takes a village," then Mary Kay is well positioned for its next fifty years because our village is growing rapidly and filled with all manner of merchants, artisans, and, yes, artists ready to link arms and stride into the twenty-first century. To illustrate my point, I would like to introduce you to one of the most talented Directors I know, Jean McMackin, and let her give you the broad strokes of how to create a successful career in Mary Kay.

Jean

Though my career as a professional artist was going well (I was represented in six galleries—four in California and two in Canada), having recently become a single mother of three teenagers, I was finding it quite challenging to make ends meet. As our situation worsened (we lost our home and were in serious debt), I was feeling hopeless and unsure of where to turn when I started praying for guidance. Little did I know at that time what God had in store for me. In fact, when He finally answered that prayer by introducing me to Mary Kay, I have to admit I was skeptical because I wasn't fond of "pushy sales people." What finally changed my mind (besides desperately needing the extra income) was the focus on teaching skin care instead of selling it. So, I agreed to try this Mary Kay thing for six months and then I'd get a "real job." Of course, before long I had begun to visualize a future in Mary Kay, and I've been chasing that dream ever since.

> I wanted to . . . devote as much time as possible to my children.

Studying the Consultant's Guide, I soon learned that, like painting, "daily effort" would be the key ingredient to my success. Early on, I developed what, in most companies, would seem like conflicting goals for my Mary Kay business. I wanted to move quickly into management to increase my income while maintaining flexibility so that I could devote as much time as possible to my children, particularly my special needs daughter who always needed help with her studies when she got home from school, as well as my painting. Fortunately, I was able to achieve both of these goals by staying true to my business mantra of "effort = results," which has served me well throughout my career.

Though I didn't know it at the time, building the level of flexibility into my life that only Mary Kay can provide became essential later in my career when I developed a neurological condition called Essential Tremor, or ET. At first it was manageable, as long as I took my medication, but as the years passed, the tremor in my hands became more and more noticeable and harder to control. Despite the recommendation of my physicians at the Tremor Clinic where I receive treatment, I had always steadfastly refused to consider surgery because, quite honestly, the idea of subjecting my brain to an invasive procedure terrified me. When my tremors reached the point where I could no longer paint, write legibly, or even use a fork, however, I finally had to face my fears and take a hard look at my treatment options.

After a great deal of research, I finally decided to undergo a procedure called Deep Brain Stimulation (DBS) in which

> I developed a neurological condition called Essential Tremor, or ET.

the surgeon attaches prongs to each hemisphere of the brain and then measures the response to electrical stimulation at various points to identify those regions that stimulate the tremors. It is a very trial-and-error type of procedure with the results being constantly monitored by a technician whose job it is to program a pacemaker-type device implanted under the skin on my chest. Though I would definitely clas-

sify DBS as "major" surgery, I am happy to report that my faith and my Mary Kay training allowed me to stay in a place of total peace throughout the procedure.

Even with all of the limitations and distractions of ET, however, I still managed to "show up" for work nearly every day and keep my Mary Kay business going. As a result, I am more committed than ever to the idea that, no

Portrait of a successful Director— Jean at Awards Night.

matter what is going on around you, consistent, daily effort is the key to achieving your goals. Sincere, focused effort rewards you with success but doesn't cost anything, and the time and energy you invest are never wasted. If I have learned nothing else through my experience, it is that prosperity lies hidden in the "daily routine" and is within easy reach for any-one willing to make some measure of effort each and every day toward a pre-determined, worthwhile goal. For me, that daily effort has resulted in sixteen appearances in the Queen's Court of Sales, qualifying for Unit Circle seventeen times, four pink Cadillacs, and, most importantly, a nomination for the annual Miss Go-Give award.

Looking back over my career, I am overwhelmed with gratitude to Mary Kay for her vision and for her willingness to pursue a dream of creating such a wonderful opportunity for women everywhere, one that can take us anywhere we want to go while creating a prosperous future for us and for our families.

It's Never Too Late

"This is the right time,
and this is the right thing."
—Thomas Moore

APPROACHING THE FINAL YEAR before my retirement, the Dingler Area made it clear that they had no intention of going out in second place. Instead, they wanted a repeat performance of the previous year when I had stepped onto the Seminar stage as Number One worldwide. So, knowing they wouldn't take "no" for an answer (just like I taught them), I rolled up my sleeves and went back to work.

Although the phrase "going out on top" had a nice ring to it, and my competitive nature probably wouldn't have let me back down anyway, I knew all too well the commitment necessary to take on such an ambitious goal. And besides, the rational part of me protested, hadn't I already climbed my mountains?

Directors arriving at my Dallas home to celebrate the Dingler Area
achieving No. One Worldwide status.

Didn't I deserve to set the cruise control on my pink Cadillac for once in my life and just enjoy the ride?

At the end of the day, however, the overriding factor was that the time just seemed so clearly "right" for me to try to retain my hard-earned title. Yes, the path was challenging, and mostly uphill, but we had already blazed the trail and even knew a few shortcuts by now. Most important, though, I had an incredible support system both at home and in the field where thousands of women were champing at the bit to prove that the Dingler Area was more than just a one-trick pony. As my son, Devin, would say, it felt like "a God thing," which meant, in the words of Don Corleone, it was an offer I couldn't refuse.

As we've learned from so many of the stories we've heard thus far, life happens to all of us and sometimes the Mary Kay philosophy has to be applied as God first, family a very close second, and career a distant third as we grapple with personal challenges that require most, if not all, of our time and energy. But when the clouds part, the traffic clears, and a road finally opens up before us, we need to be ready to seize the moment and pursue those dreams that have been waiting oh so patiently for that "right" moment to come along. Setting an example of just how to carpe that diem, former Dingler Area Director Kellye Conley endured years of detours, stalls, and sudden stops before finally finding herself in the right place at the right time and, of course, in the right company to pursue her dreams.

Kellye

I was eighteen years old when I started my Mary Kay business. Well, the first time anyway. My parents would laugh and say "we can always tell when her car payment is due . . . she heads out the back door with those pink bags over her shoulder." I did manage to make some car payments on that first attempt but gradually eased out of the business as I found love, got married, had two beautiful children, and started working (more than) a full-time job. In fact, when I was presented with the Mary Kay opportunity a second time,

> **I was finally able to experience the dream of seeing my kids get off the school bus every day.**

I was living out of a suitcase, and trying to cover a twenty-six state territory while still being some kind of mom to my two- and three-year-old children and wife to my poor husband.

Even though I had been praying for a change, I resisted joining Mary Kay a second time due to my prior history. I finally heard God's still small voice through the din of my negative self-talk, however, and had to admit that this was the answer to those prayers I'd been sending up. So, I said "yes" to a better future and made a pact with myself that, this time, I would do it Mary Kay's way.

Well, Mary Kay must have known what she was talking about because by the end of that first year, I had left my job and gained a car. Not a bad trade. I was finally able to experience the dream of seeing my kids get off the school bus every day and scheduling my business around my family's needs instead of the other way around. Diligently working my business week in and week out, this time I was doing far more than making car payments, and, when I was finally able to attend my first Seminar, it was to debut as a new Director.

My wonderful new Unit worked hard and stayed focused so we could complete our first Unit Club just two years later.

As proud as I was to represent our Unit on the Seminar stage, however, I was even more excited to be asked to speak at the Directors' meeting by my National, Doretha Dingler. Everything seemed to be going as well as I could have ever hoped for, but, even though I left Seminar that year with new goals and dreams like everyone else, my goals just wouldn't seem to take root. I couldn't reignite the spark, the passion I had felt when I was working for that first car and to spend time with my family. I finally had to admit that I was, well, satisfied. I was happy right where I was, and no matter how many ambitious goals I tried to set for myself, my heart just wasn't in it. I simply wasn't ready yet.

Well, I guess God decided if I wasn't going to challenge myself then he would take up the slack. First, I received a surprise visit from the stork. He brought me a beautiful baby boy who was perfect in every way except for one tiny little ear that somehow went missing. He also had a little trouble with the umbilical cord on his way out and had to stay in the hospital a few extra days until they finally let him come home with a couple of follow-up appointments scheduled at Childrens' Hospital. Nothing I couldn't handle.

> God decided if I wasn't going to challenge myself then he would take up the slack.

Then, my first day out with our new baby, I received an urgent call from my husband saying, "Come and get me, I just cut my thumb off." By the time I could get there, however, the ambulance had already taken him to the Louisville Hand Clinic for emergency surgery.

Luckily, they were able to save his thumb, but no sooner had that crisis passed than he informed me that his grandparents would be moving in with us. Now, our house was not built to accommodate two families, and I wasn't sure I was either. I had a new baby and an injured husband, both of whom required a seemingly endless series of medical appointments, and would now be responsible for taking care of two elderly people with whom I would be living in close quarters. Thank God I was able to keep working my Mary Kay business while I worked around all of these new "opportunities" in my life.

For the next several years, I continued to take care of my business and my family, never missing a Mary Kay event or a medical appointment, but I still felt like something wasn't quite right. How could I have had a dream that I was so absolutely passionate about and then never have another? It seemed like my dream machine was broken. I mean, who wouldn't want more money, diamonds, cars, free trips, etc., and yet I just couldn't picture myself as a top Director, much less a National, nor find the motivation to get there.

How could I have a dream that I was so absolutely passionate about and then never have another?

I didn't have long to reflect on such matters, though, as my son began the series of constructive surgeries for his missing ear, four in California and one in Virginia. The medical expenses were daunting enough, but, because we lived in Kentucky, the additional travel costs created a significant financial challenge. I eventually decided to accept a full-time job that had been offered to me during this difficult time, with the idea that we would have better insurance to help with all of the surgeries. I figured I could do anything for a year or two if it would help my little guy get a new ear.

So, I sat my Unit down and gave them the plan. I would continue to hold Unit meetings, service my customers, work a full-time job, see to my kids' activities, and keep the books for my husband's contracting business. No problem. Except that it took almost an entire year before the surgeries began and then we had to hit the road every three or four months. The trips and the surgeries went well, however, and we felt God's hand on us every step of the way, but, as everything began to pile up, I found it harder and harder to keep up the pace. Fortunately, we were in the home stretch leading up to the final surgery so the finish line was in sight. Or so I thought.

> While we were recovering from my son's third procedure and preparing for his fourth, we received devastating news.

While we were recovering from my son's third procedure and preparing for his fourth, we received devastating news: my seventeen-year-old daughter had been diagnosed with thyroid cancer and would need surgery and radiation treatment immediately. Ever the devoted sister, she actually flew to California to support her brother during his surgery and then flew home early to have hers. But that was only the beginning.

My daughter did not respond well to the initial treatments, and the cancer soon spread to her lymph nodes. Altogether she has undergone three surgeries, two I-131 treatments, and thirty external beam radiation treatments. As if that weren't enough, during this time she moved away to begin college at the University of Kentucky to pursue her own dream of becoming a civil engineer. Despite her doctor's recommendation that she stay home for a semester because the radiation treatments would mean she couldn't eat, drink, or swallow and would be in constant pain, my amazing daughter never even missed a class, finishing the semester with all As and Bs. She maintained a positive attitude throughout this ordeal and never wavered in her determination, all of which I attribute to her faith and to being raised in a Mary Kay home.

As you can imagine, my Mary Kay business was relegated to the back burner during this period, and I began to question

Teaching a class with Kellye.

what I was doing with my life. Ironically, I had lots of time to think and pray about things because my corporate job required me to drive three to five hundred miles per week.

I would think about all the different things I could do with my life: what businesses I could start, what degrees I could pursue, etc., etc. No matter what plan I came up with, however, nothing compared with the Mary Kay opportunity. I

Why wouldn't I work just as hard for myself and travel the world?

was earning a good salary and could count on a one to four percent raise every year, but I knew that I could earn that same money in about half the time with Mary Kay and give myself a raise any time I wanted. I just kept thinking, *If I'm willing to work this hard for someone else, constantly traveling for a job where I could be let go at anytime, why wouldn't I work just as hard for myself and travel the world, all-expenses paid, with my husband?* It was like God just let me drive and drive until I was ready to truly listen to the plan he had in store for me. It took going back to the corporate world, where I could truly empathize with all of those women with whom I came into contact who were miserable in their jobs, to fully appreciate the value of the Mary Kay opportunity and to recapture that dream I had been seeking for so long. I thought I was working for the insurance, but, as it turns out, God sent me there for inspiration, and I came back with plenty. I was finally ready to dream a bigger dream.

Returning from what I now call my "Mary Kay sabbatical," I received tremendous support from my loyal Unit members and from my Senior Director and future National as I worked to rebuild my business. Then, six months after moving Mary Kay squarely back onto the front burner, my daughter was able to enroll in an insurance plan offered by the university, and I left my job the same day.

Today, I am happy to report that, along with earning nine cars and various other awards, we have qualified for Unit Circle to celebrate the Mary Kay fiftieth anniversary and will be debuting our first Directors at Seminar. These days, I am doing more than just dreaming and can visualize myself someday becoming a National Sales Director. I am so thankful for God's perfect plan and the opportunity to share the "gift" of Mary Kay with as many women as possible so they too can follow their dreams when the time is right.

Losing Your Way to Success

*"He is no fool who gives what he cannot keep
to gain that which he cannot lose."*
—JIM ELLIOT

I WAS HOLDING ON FOR DEAR LIFE, praying I would survive this encounter with the thousand pound beast now stamping its feet and baring large, yellow teeth at me. Of course, Mary Kay wasn't faring any better trying to ride her camel, so at least I was in good company. This was just one of many adventures we had on our Top Ten trip to the Middle East, and it was, to say the least, unforgettable. It was also a reminder of how far I had come, literally and figuratively, from my small town Texas roots. Bruce and I might have eventually gotten around to visiting some of the destinations on those Top Ten itineraries, but we would never have booked the kind of five-star accommodations that were standard when traveling

With Bruce (and a new friend) in Egypt.

Mary Kay learning to ride a camel.

with Mary Kay. Besides the opportunities to travel, though, it was the confidence and self-esteem I had acquired that were Mary Kay's most valuable gift. I doubt that girl from Athens, Texas, would ever have even approached a camel, much less ridden one. The same goes for bartering with local merchants in Venice, visiting mainland China, and asking strange men in Athens, Greece, where they bought their underwear (but that's another story altogether).

Just like the proverbial journey of a thousand miles, our Mary Kay journey started with a single step. And then another, and another, until we were standing on the Seminar stage as successful Consultants, Directors, Senior Directors, and, for some of us, Nationals. We learned, and practiced, those fundamental lessons until our skills, and our confidence, allowed us to move up to the next level. A funny thing happened as our Mary Kay businesses improved, however. Our personal lives improved as well. We asked for more and put up with less as we began to discover our true self-worth. You've already heard from women who left intolerable situations, both personally and professionally, as their Mary Kay training took root and allowed them to

catch a glimpse of what they could achieve and the person they could become.

We've seen that lan-guage, shyness, fear, and, yes, even family, can all be overcome if someone is simply willing to fol-low the steps as Mary

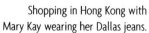
Shopping in Hong Kong with Mary Kay wearing her Dallas jeans.

Kay laid them down over fifty years ago. Then, like a rising tide that lifts all boats, we will find every aspect of our lives improving as we come into our own. Sometimes, though, it's hard to measure those intangible personal benefits we're receiving as we work on our professional development. But not in Barbara Yerdon's case. She can tell you exactly how much Mary Kay helped to improve her life in a very personal way, and I'll bet many of you out there can relate to this story of how one woman balanced the scales and forged a new path to success and personal well-being.

My Mary Kay journey began reluctantly. I had promised a friend that I would go with her to a skin care class, but, when the day came, I most definitely did not want to go. After all, my "skin care" routine consisted of little more than a wet

Barbara before . . .

. . . and after.

washcloth, and what little glamour I wore, if any, came from the dollar store. Growing up on a farm as one of ten siblings, I was raised to be frugal so the prospect of buying makeup or skin care products seemed like an unnecessary luxury even as an adult. I was also raised to keep my word, however, so, having told my friend that I would be there, I felt I had no choice but to keep the appointment.

I dutifully tried the skin care products the hostess offered to me, wanting to be polite, and to my complete surprise, I loved them! I ended up buying every-thing and even booked an appointment for a second facial. I told the Consult-ant "I want everything, I should just do this." Happy to oblige, the Consultant gave me everything I needed to know

I also had a weight problem, and that made me extremely self-conscious.

about the Company and invited me to be a special guest at an event the following Saturday. When I got there, everyone was having so much fun that I just wanted to be a part of it. I finally turned to my Consultant and asked, "Where do I sign?"

Once the excitement wore off, however, I started to get a little nervous. Though I've always had an outgoing personality, I also had a weight problem, and that made me extremely self-conscious about getting up in front of people. Fortunately, I had a large family, so I was hoping I could support a small business just taking care of them. With the encouragement and support of my Director, Hellen Brook-shire, however, I finally started to move out of that comfort zone as my confidence grew along with a desire to do, and be, more. Patient but persistent, I was finally able to start believing in myself.

I was married with both a full and part-time job when I started out in Mary Kay, and, because my large extended family has always been very close, I was constantly doing something with or for my mom, dad, siblings, nieces, and nephews. With all that I had going on already, adding a new business may not have looked like the best decision at the time, except that Mary Kay didn't feel like an extra "job." I was spending time with people I enjoyed, teaching women how to use a great product, and all the while gaining confidence in my newfound abilities. As it turns out, growing up on a farm was the perfect preparation for my new career. Hard work? A large extended (Mary Kay) family? I felt right at home.

> When I went to Unit meetings, I would always sit in the back.

Change is always difficult, however. When I went to Unit meetings, I would always sit in the back, afraid that I would be called upon to come up front. Well, one day it finally happened when I was asked to do the features and benefits for a product the following week. I was in a panic, wishing I could say "no" and trying to think of every reason in the world to get out of it, but, as usual, that old do-the-right-thing gene kicked in, and I showed up as promised. Of course, once I began to talk, I started to stutter. My hands were shaking, my palms were sweating, and the more nervous I got, the more I stuttered, shook, and sweated. It took everything I had to keep from crying and running out, but I got through it. And then, when it was over, I wanted to do it again because I knew I could do better.

A short while later, as I was building my business and my confidence, our Unit put on a special event. The guest speaker that day talked about driving to the cemetery when she earned her first pink Cadillac so she could visit her father's grave. While I listened, the tears poured down my face because my own father had recently been diagnosed with cancer and wasn't doing well. At the time, I only had one team member, but, after hearing that emotional talk and thinking about my dad, I made the decision then and there to earn my first car and make my parents proud while there was still time. Four months later, I was not only driving that car but had finished Director qualification as well. Best of all, Mom and Dad were both sitting proudly in the audience for my debut.

A few years later, however, I went to the hospital with what I thought was a migraine headache and learned there was a cyst blocking my spinal fluid. They kept me in the hospital for four weeks on a morphine drip that rendered me unable to function and then, even when I finally got to go home, I had to remain on a high dosage of medication for two months. Of course, having taken so much time off as a new Director, my production had dropped to the point that I was barely making it. During my recovery, I

> They kept me in the hospital for four weeks on a morphine drip.

tried working from home to rebuild my business, but it was a struggle. Ultimately, I had to have a conversation with my National, Doretha Dingler, about resigning my Directorship.

I cried as I wrestled with this difficult decision but knew I needed to concentrate on getting healthy. Then one day, arriving home after a doctor's appointment, I found myself listening to a voicemail left by someone at Mary Kay corporate saying they hoped I would get well soon. That, along with flowers and tons of cards from Mary Kay ladies all over the United States, most of whom I had never even met, made me feel so blessed to be part of such an amazing and caring Company. And I needed every bit of that support a short time later when I had to attend my first meeting as a Red Jacket instead of a Director. Ironically, I found it difficult to just be sitting in the audience when, not so very long ago, I had been praying no one would ask me to stand up and come to the front of the room where I now felt I belonged. Fortunately, another character trait my parents instilled in me was persistence (some might say stubbornness). I loved my business, my Mary Kay family, and the Company too much to give up now, and if that meant starting over, then so be it.

> I decreased my dress size to the tune of a hundred and thirty-five pounds!

Two years later, I once again debuted as a Director and a member of the Mary Kay Honor Society. This time, however, I felt like more than just a new Director, I felt like a new me. And for good reason. Even though I had to reclaim the position, I hadn't lost the hard-won confidence and self-esteem I had acquired through my Mary Kay training. In fact, as I worked to increase my business, I decreased my dress size—to the tune of a hundred and thirty-five pounds! All that extra weight that had dogged me my entire adult life, literally weighing down my self-esteem, was now a thing of the past. Let me tell you, the only thing that feels better than wearing a smaller dress size is wearing a smaller Director's suit!

I've hit a few bumps in the road since that second debut, but the Company graciously agreed to work with me the few times I needed it, and I've never looked back. To-date I've earned five Mary Kay cars, qualified for Queen's Court of Sales, and had a career-high one-month commission check over $3,600. Before Mary Kay, I had never left my home

With "Before" Barbara at Seminar.

state of New York, but now I've traveled all over the country (including eighteen trips to Dallas). Though I kept my full-time job throughout all of the ups and downs, this year the company is being sold, after which I will be working my Mary Kay career full-time as I pursue my dream of becoming a National Sales Director. These days, I simply could not imagine a life without my Mary Kay family, and I thank God for putting such amazing women in my path.

Where I Finished

*"Don't cry because it's over,
smile because it happened."*

—DR. SUESS (THEODOR SUESS GEISEL)

I WAS FINISHED. THE DECISION WAS FINAL, and there was no one to whom I could appeal. Keeping a stiff upper lip, I tried to face the end with dignity as two men in dark suits escorted me to my final destination. Of course, the applause helped to lift my spirits as I stepped onto the stage to make my farewell speech at Leadership Conference on the eve of my retirement.

Looking back over the stories that have been told in this book, and those of the thousands of other women I've known during the course of my Mary Kay career, I consider myself truly blessed. Though I have certainly had my challenges, along with the usual ups and downs that come with living a full life, I realize there are so

Returning to our Dallas home.

many women who have had to overcome obstacles I couldn't even dream of. And those are the stories I wanted you to hear.

Yes, I managed, with the hard work and support of the entire Dingler Area, to retire as Number One worldwide, and I will always be very proud of that accomplishment. But I am also well aware that I did so standing on the shoulders of all those women who were "just working their Mary Kay" as they struggled with a personal or family medical issue, raising children as a single mother, deciding whether to leave a difficult relationship, or just the normal fear and self-esteem demons that plague every one of us. All those women gave just a little bit more and worked just little bit harder (or in some cases, quite a bit harder) to help the Dingler Area go out as Number One.

Because of the hard work and dedication of the Dingler Area, I was able to achieve such milestones as being the first to earn over $100,000 in commissions in one month and being the fifth NSD, out of only seven, to have reached the pinnacle of the sales force by attaining the Number One position nationally. As a result of these accomplishments, I have received a lot of formal recognition from Mary Kay the company, from having my portraits hung in the Hall of Fame and Hall of Honor to seeing my legacy, as well as those of the other Mary Kay pioneers, memorialized in a unique multimedia display recently unveiled at Mary Kay headquarters in Dallas. And though I encourage those of you attending Seminar to take the official tour of headquarters, where you can see firsthand the incredi-

Jennifer Cook

ble job that Executive Support and Museum Director Jennifer Cook has done keeping our rich Mary Kay heritage alive, that is only part of the story.

With the benefit of perfect hindsight, I now realize that it is Mary Kay the community that has allowed one woman's dream to enrich the lives of women for the past fifty years and that will allow her legacy to live on for the next fifty, or a hundred, or two hundred years, or, as Mary Kay herself would say,

> Our culture . . . tends to create an "up or out" mentality.

"as long as women have skin." Thus, I feel it is important that we take a moment to recognize all of those unsung heroes out there who are quietly weaving the fabric of the Mary Kay community for the next generation.

My purpose in writing this book was not to hold out a few women as being somehow more worthy of recognition than their peers, but rather to present them as representatives of the (now) millions of women who are, or one day may be, in their shoes. Our culture, though it rewards entrepreneurs like Mary Kay who are willing to risk forging a new path or creating a new product, also tends to create an "up or out" mentality. We feel that if we are not moving "up," whatever that means, at the same rate as our peers that we are somehow failing and will soon find ourselves out of favor, out of opportunities for advancement, and, ultimately, "out" of a job.

Though corporate culture is improving generally, with the expansion of flexible work hours and guaranteed family leave time, the "fast track" is still reserved for those who can show up and commit the lion's share of their time and energy to the "J-O-B." And that's in the progressive, leading edge work environment of the United States. In many of the world markets where Mary Kay now has a presence, particularly in developing countries, if a woman can even get a professional level corporate job, she certainly won't receive any accommodation to shoulder the additional responsibilities traditionally placed on women the world over. Mary Kay understood from personal experience the dilemma faced by women in the workforce and therefore designed her "track to run on" with several lanes to allow for the realities that women face as they juggle all of the responsibilities heaped on them by their families, society, and, of course, themselves.

The women we've heard from in these pages, and all those they represent, prove that Mary Kay was right when she bet on the potential of women if they were just provided with the right kind of opportunity, the kind that allowed for life to go up, down, or sideways, and still not be "out" of luck when it came to having a career. In order to believe that opportunity truly exists, however, most women have to hear it for themselves. And that's why these "I" stories, and the millions just

> Mary Kay was right when she bet on the potential of women.

like them that are happening as we speak, must continue to be told. Primitive cultures have a tradition of handing down oral histories from one generation to the next so important lessons are not lost and the community can continue to thrive by repeating the successes, and avoiding the mistakes, of their ancestors. The Mary Kay community is not so very different as we help one another find the shortcuts and avoid the pitfalls of life and business through our "I" stories.

So, as the band strikes up for one more rousing chorus of "It's not where you start, it's where you finish," I have to say that if I have in fact finished (and after two books, my family has their doubts), it is in a place of gratitude. A place of appreciation for every woman who helped me reach my goals by not quitting when things got tough and by continuing to believe in herself when that old nemesis self-doubt reared its ugly head. Earlier I told you about the termination letter that almost had me singing, "I was finished before I started," but though it pales in comparison to the challenges I would face later in my career, I can tell you from countless conversations with those who have heard me speak that far more people remember the fact I was almost terminated than recall the number of times our Area generated over $67 million in annual

> Far more people remember the fact I was almost terminated.

production or that we developed nineteen National Sales Directors. Having these accolades was an honor and a privilege, but no one cares about my ten million in career earnings if her husband won't watch the kids so she can attend a Unit meeting. As I've no doubt told you many times by now, the magic of Mary Kay is that it can meet you where you are, but it's better if that meeting happens face-to-face with someone who has actually been there and can show you the way forward.

Happily relaxing.

This book will have achieved its aim if it merely keeps the conversation going. Yes, we want to hear about the Barbara Sundens out there smashing company records year after year, making an indelible contribution to the legacies of Mary Kay, the Dingler Area, and now the Sunden Area while proving once again that, above all, the Mary Kay opportunity is unlimited. But let's not let those stories, as inspiring as they are, overshadow the Mildred Caldwells. Women who, before they found Mary Kay, may have been wondering how they were going to survive as a single mother and praying for a miracle. Fortunately, that miracle was delivered not by one angel, but by many. For, as Mary Kay liked to remind visitors to her office when she gave them a little cherub engraved with her favorite quote by Lucretius: *"We are each of us angels with only one wing; we can only fly by embracing one another."*

Celebrating my retirement with Bruce.

$10,000,000

**MARY KAY INC.
MILLIONAIRES CLUB
Award Of Achievement**
Presented To

DORETHA DINGLER

To Acknowledge Her
**OUTSTANDING CAREER
EARNINGS ACCOMPLISHMENT
LEADERSHIP 2003**

MARY KAY INC.

Proudly Recognizes
Executive National Sales Director

Doretha Dingler

*for achieving outstanding area
performance of*

$66,700,000

Seminar 2002

NATIONAL
News Notes

Doretha Dingler does it again!
Records are made to be broken.

Independent Executive National Sales Director Doretha Dingler has broken the NSD monthly commission record for a second time. She earned an incredible $104,000 in the month of September! That's the highest monthly commission in Company history and it beats her own record of $97,000 that she set last year.

NATIONAL
News Notes
NSD INNER CIRCLE RECOGNITION

ON-TARGET INNER CIRCLE

On-Target for $1,000,000
Doretha Dingler

For commission totaling
one million in one year

Excerpts from "National News Notes."

Enjoying my Scottsdale retreat.

Some of my favorite photos with Mary Kay.

133

United States

Canada

DINGLER

Philippines

Brazil

AREA

Mexico

Korea

#1 WORLDWIDE

Czech Republic

2003

England

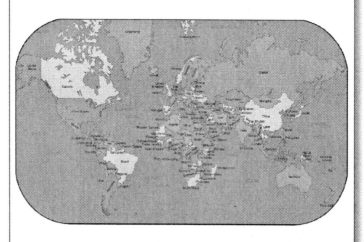

At the time of her retirement, Doretha's area was
represented in all 50 states and multiple countries.
She was one of only five Independent National Sales
Directors to have ever held the title of #1 Worldwide
in the 40-year history of Mary Kay.

Acknowledgments

IRST AND FOREMOST, I'd like to thank my husband, Bruce, who has been as supportive of me in writing this book as he was throughout my Mary Kay career (if not more so since technically I'm now "retired"). Likewise, I would like to thank my son, Devin, his wife, Sandra, and our granddaughter, Brittany, who have contributed their time, effort, creativity, and emotional support throughout this project. Once the book was written, I became indebted to my editor, Candace Johnson, who makes me sound good, and to my designers and magicians, Carol and Gary Rosenberg, who make me look good. Of course, I am eternally grateful to all my contributors, many of whom are included in this book, who so generously shared their personal stories with me. Finally, a special thanks to Jennifer Cook, Erma Thomson, and Yvonne Pendleton, who graciously agreed to share their insights and recollections of working with Mary Kay Ash for many years.

Afterword

Having been a successful newspaper editor in Dallas for many years before taking the job at Mary Kay's corporate headquarters, I was aware that most people had no idea what was going on within the walls of that shiny gold building on Stemmons (I-35) Freeway—not to mention in the lives of millions of women around the world. I said that to anyone who'd listen at the Company, and made it my goal to instill the larger message into every writing assignment I had in *Applause* and *Director's Memo* that first year. It might be a story about a woman who was forced by her company's mandatory office hours to drop off her children at the bus stop and leave them there alone so she could get to work on time. And the larger story that finding work flexibility in her Mary Kay business solved what had been her greatest angst. Or an independent sales director who found the son she'd given up for adoption in large part because he had married a sales director, who encouraged him to never give up on his dream of finding his mother. The stories and their larger message were endless.

The way that Mary Kay believed in women long before they had the confidence to believe in themselves is a story of magnificent proportions—one that speaks volumes about how

Mary Kay is about much more than cosmetics. She had been a single mother in an inflexible, unappreciative workplace. Providing women a better way to accomplish their life's goals was what made Mary Kay the proudest. I heard countless stories about women Mary Kay had counseled to cut back on their career during a family crisis—"your Mary Kay business will be here for you when your circumstances allow." She worried about women pressured to sacrifice family for business. And, while delighted that professional women with college degrees were clamoring for the flexibility and income potential of a Mary Kay business, she made it clear the opportunity needed to be right for them—especially the people aspects of it. She didn't care if you had run a large division of an automobile manufacturer, could you sell a lipstick and furthermore, could you inspire other women to do so? And then could you help them achieve their dreams each step of the way.

One year when she visited the New Sales Director class touring Dallas headquarters, Mary Kay learned of a medical doctor who was an Independent Sales Director. Impressed as she was, Mary Kay's note to me said it all. Keep an eye on the doctor, she told me. If she continues to do well with her Mary Kay business, it would merit a story. While the fact that she was a doctor was impressive, it wasn't pertinent to the independent sales force *unless* and *until* the doctor found the Mary Kay experience provided her with whatever it was that medicine had not. It did and we wrote the story of the doctor who traded her stethoscope for a beauty case while volunteering at a health clinic to put her medical knowledge to good use.

Women like Doretha Dingler also made a lasting impression on me. Though she is one of the most successful independent businesswomen in Mary Kay sales force history,

Doretha's story is symbolic of what a woman can achieve when you give her a track to run on.

I will always treasure having the opportunity to understand Mary Kay from the lady herself in her last decade of life, when she fully understood the meaning of her life's work as the world began to recognize and applaud her. The woman that had long been portrayed as a big-haired blonde Texan who encouraged prayer and songs at her business meetings was coming into her own as the "greatest female entrepreneur" and one of the "greatest business stories" of our time.

As the company she founded celebrates half a century, I take such great pride that I was able to get to know a woman who is virtually all by herself in the category of inspirational business leaders with an innate understanding of women.

—Yvonne Pendleton

During her nearly twenty years at Mary Kay, Yvonne Pendleton was director of corporate heritage, academic outreach, and executive speechwriting. She worked closely with Mary Kay Ash and was with her in her office the day Mary Kay first fell ill and subsequently suffered the stroke that would rob her of her voice. In addition to writing for and with Mary Kay Ash, she worked with Executive Chairman Richard Rogers upon his return to the Company in 2000, as well as Mary Kay's grandson and current company executive, Ryan Rogers. During her tenure, Yvonne wrote for every chief executive and every president in the history of Mary Kay, including those who hold the titles now.

Yvonne Pendleton

About the Author

Doretha Dingler is a Mary Kay Elite Executive Independent National Sales Director Emeritus. Coming from humble beginnings bidding peas for her family's east Texas agribusiness, Doretha eventually rose to the position of National Sales Director with Mary Kay, overseeing a multi-million dollar international cosmetics enterprise and proving that the opportunity created by Mary Kay Ash when she founded her company in the early sixties was not only real but available to any woman from any background. Joining the company shortly after it was founded, Doretha worked closely with Mary Kay from the Company's early years until her passing in 2001 and still considers her the most significant role model for women in business today. Doretha still devotes time to writing, teaching, and encouraging others to continue Mary Kay's priceless legacy of empowering women.